359.96
DEC

D0760526

FIRST BLACK MARINES
Vanguard of a Legacy

Fred deClouet

OCEANSIDE PUBLIC LIBRARY

3 1232 00477 5658

TO SOW THE FALLOW SOIL James C. Winston
Publishing Company, Inc.

Trade Division of Winston-Derek Publishers Group, Inc.

OCEANSIDE PUBLIC LIBRARY
330 N. Coast Highway
Oceanside, CA 92054

© 1995 by James C. Winston Publishing Company, Inc.
         Trade Division of Winston-Derek Publishers Group, Inc.

All rights reserved. No part of this book may be reproduced in any form without written permission from the publishers, except by a reviewer who may quote brief passages in a review to be printed in a newspaper or magazine.

First printing

PUBLISHED BY JAMES C. WINSTON PUBLISHING COMPANY, INC.
Nashville, Tennessee 37205

Library of Congress Catalog Card No: 93-60354
ISBN: 1-55523-618-9

Printed in the United States of America

DEC 27 1996

To all Marines who have served in World War II and beyond, particularly those who served with the 51st Defense Battalion.

Contents

Preface

Since the main thrust of this book is concerned with individual memories spanning some fifty years—and it is reasonable to expect less than 100% recall—there undoubtedly will be statements made with more vigor than coherence and with conflicting interpretations.

The writer therefore feels obligated to provide the reader with accurate and unbiased historical facts that could serve as a kind of gyroscopic beacon for keeping this treatise in perspective.

This was made possible by two highly regarded Marine Corps historians who gave me permission to quote freely from their outstanding book, *Blacks in the Marine Corps*.

Mr. Henry I. Shaw, Jr., who is the Chief Historian of the History and Museums Division, a graduate of Hope College, he obtained his masters in history at Colombia University. A Marine veteran of World War II and Korea, he has written extensively on Marine operation in the modern era. Mr. Ralph W. Donnelly, Assistant Head of the Reference Section, is a graduate of Wilson Teacher's College who received his MA in political science from Catholic University. He has had a varied career as school teacher, insurance executive and official historian and is a widely published writer on historical subjects.

Fred deClouet

Acknowledgements

No book can come into being without acquiring debts along the way. This one is most heavily indebted to Mr. Gene Doughty, National President of the Montford Point Marine Association, Inc.

From the first day when I called Gene and briefed him on what I wanted to do and asked for his help, his response was a very positive and enthusiastic: "Yes! Yes! Yes!" Several days later I received a letter from Gene outlining a plan of action for the research that would be required. His invaluable help in so many ways has been a sustaining and much needed factor throughout the development of this book.

I am grateful to Mr. Henry I. Shaw, Chief Historian of the History and Museum Division of the Marine Corps Historical Center.

I would be amiss if I did not thank the many friends who aided me with research, locating the Marines who were an essential element in this work, and persuading them to participate in this project.

I owe an especially strong thanks to Leota Fox, my wife, who patiently devoted hours on the computer writing drafts of the original manuscript and trying to educate me on computer capabilities.

Many thanks to Judy Helton, a computer expert, for helping me to prepare the manuscript for the publisher.

Looking back to 1942 when I first met most of the men listed below, I am always amazed at how fortunate I was to have been accepted and helped by them. It is doubtful that I would have made it through the Marine Corps without their help.

Academically, they were all at the very least, high school graduates. Many had college degrees, a few post graduate degrees.

It was awesome and intimidating, but inspiring, to have the opportunity and privilege to be in such illustrious company. Here I was, Fred deClouet, whose brief encounter with the academic world did not extend beyond the sixth grade, somehow appearing on equal footing with these giants. A miracle, I thought.

I know, without a doubt, that this book would not have reached the conceptual stage without having known these men. It would take more than one lifetime to thank them for not only being central players in the scenario, but for being a major influence in how I have tried to live my life as well.

I am very pleased to be able to say that every one of these names listed here has a face that shall be forever etched in my memory. Unfortunately, many names had to be omitted because of space requirements. I thank them all.

Alexander, Lewis M. Jr.
Allain, Joseph M. Jr.
Anderson, Charles E.
Bankhead, Woodrow W.
Bates, Walter Jr.
Bostic, Arnold R.
Boxill, John
Braxton, Edward H.
Brazil, William H.
Brewer, Herbert L.
Broyard, Samuel A.
Burns, Leonard L.
Bynes, Salomon
Cancler, John W. Jr.
Canns, Julius D.
Carothers, John L.
Carr, Earl W.
Cash, George T.

Clayton, James L.
Cooper, Melvin
Cuffee, Leslie A
Curry, Ernest
Culp, Edward A.
Davis, Edgar Jr.
Des Vigne, Sidney L. Jr.
Dobard, Morris E. Jr.
Duncan, Paul D.
Eldridge, Myles L. Jr.
Evans, William L.
Fraser, Gilbert Jr.
Faison, Percy H. Jr.
Fizer, Edwin J. Jr.
Floyd, Raymond B.
Givens, Other L.
Gordon, Isaac B.
Gray, Charles A.
Griffin, Ezekial B. Jr.
Griffin, William B.
Guillebaux, Charles G.
Hamner, Lee
Harris, Jones D.
Harris, Price B.
Haselrig, Burrell L. Jr.
Hayward, Charles R.
Henderson, Finis E. Jr.
Hubbard, William G.
Huff, Edgar R.
Johnson, Horace D.
Latimer, Reaster
LeBlanc A.J.

Ledeaux, Anderson T.

Lewis, John D.

Lipscomb, Edward I.

Mahon, Dynecourt

Martin, Clarence P.

Morrow, Harold A.

Muldro, Alfonso D.

Nunn, Paul

Orr, William H. Jr.

Owens, Fred E.

Parks, Robert S. Jr.

Perry, Howard P.

Richardson, Hayward W.

Rochon, Leo H.

Simmons, Frank

Spears, Leon N.

Smith (Smittie) Poker Player, never knew his first name.
   Chicago

Tate, Victor E.

Thompson, Sinkfield

Tillman, John E. L.

Wade, Louise R.

Whitlock, Kenneth E.

Williams, Irving L.

Wright, Harry L.

Introduction

The contributors of the various chapters of this momentous collection have, through the author, made every effort to provide the reader with flashes of fear, heartache, accomplishment, anguish, defeat and triumph of the first Black men in the United States Marine Corps. The question might justifiably be advanced as to why has the author waited until fifty years expired before attempting such an inspiring and salient chronicle? Fred deClouet, one of the twenty-three of us who left from New Orleans, Louisiana in September of 1942 to become an active element of the historic first Black Marines, has often given answer to such inquiry with the statement, "It takes time for even conspicuous events to become impressive history." He has perpetually agonized over the fact that even at the present time there are those in America who have no knowledge of Black men having served in the U.S. Marine Corps for as long as they have or of their involvement in World War II.

Each individual participated in his assigned duty, had his personal reasons for volunteering to serve his country, protected his own self-respect, and made every effort to help fellow Marines to protect theirs. It is indeed understandable that with the passing of nearly fifty years since the herein reported experiences unfolded into realities, aroused emotions have quieted, wounds have healed to limited extents, but some never-to-be accepted events and regulations will continue to agonize the hearts and minds of former Black Marines until buried with them in their graves.

One can easily follow up on the above allegation when reflecting upon such facts as the Commandant of the Marine Corps, at that time, openly objecting to Negroes entering the Marine Corps because he believed that such men could not satisfactorily perform. It was Eleanor Roosevelt who carried the colors for positive action. President Franklin Roosevelt approved of her actions and signed the order.

In order to substantially reduce the anticipated wretchedness, and possible martyrdom that may have occurred if Black Marines had been ordered to Camp LeJeune, the Federal Statute was adhered to and Montford Point was hurriedly thrown together. As each hut was completed, twelve more Black men became unwanted constituents of the United States Marines.

It should be said at this point that most of the White officers and White enlisted NCO's made an effort to accommodate a group of Black men who were determined to be not just Marines, but great U.S. Marines. There were exceptions, as may have been expected, but it has now been accepted that men of Montford Point were darn good Marines.

It was the good fortune of this writer to be assigned to the 9th Platoon along with Edgar Huff, (better known now as Sergeant Major Huff) who was able to overcome academic limitations and to become a hero and living legendary figure in the U.S. Marine Corps about whom much is said in this book.

The terminologies Black, White, Negro, Colored, are very frequently used throughout the duration of this report primarily because they represent the thinking and circumstance of the period about which this is written. With deep regret it is recognized that most of these terms and others have continued in use today when referring to inhabitants of our country instead of the singular term "American." Remaining within the tradition, this section is brought to a proud close with a statement quoted from comments in this historical report by Gunnery Sergeant, Perry E. Fischer, Montford Point Camp, 8th Marine Ammunition Company, U.S. Marines 1940–1946, who happens to be White:

These men who worked, fought, were wounded, and died under the American Flag, who had been treated as second class citizens all their lives, had to fight segregation to get into the Marine Corps so that they could fight the enemies of America. They did this while still stereotyped as second class citizens, but they showed that they were 1st Class Americans in the jungles of the Solomon Islands, on the beaches of Saipan, Tinian, Guam, Pelilieu, on the sand of Iwo Jima, and on the heights of Okinawa.

As the 21st Century approaches, may we reflect upon the progress of America and the contribution of Black men associated with this growth and development. Black Marines who were not fortunate to return to their families, cry out from their graves to their younger counterparts to cast aside the paths of self-destruction brought forth by habits of drugs, crime, and low self-esteem, and follow the narrow channels of determined success and respectful achievement as demonstrated by the Black Marines of Montford Point about whom you will read in chapters to follow.

The author has exhibited the possession of many employable skills and knowledge since returning to civilian life, not the least of which is this well documented legacy of the first Black Marines.

Dr. Raymond B. Floyd

A Select Few

"If what I saw today [Negroes in U.S. Marine Corps uniforms] is any indication of how the war is going, America is in deep trouble." These words spoken by a member of an exclusive upper midwestern country club and heard by a black employee essentially summed up the sentiments of many Americans in 1942. For it was the first time in its history the Marine Corps had decided to open its doors to Negroes.

On June 25, 1941, President Franklin D. Roosevelt issued Executive Order No. 8802 establishing the Fair Employment Practices Commission with a statement that said:

> In affirming the policy of full participation in the defense program by all persons regardless of race, creed or national origin, and directing certain action in furtherance of said policy . . . All departments of the government including the Armed Forces, shall lead the way in erasing discrimination over color or race.[1]

Under the direction of Major General Commandant Thomas Holcomb steps were taken to comply with the President's Executive Order. The order was unpopular at headquarters,

Marine Corps. Blacks simply could not meet the high standard of the Marine Corps, it was argued. The commandant himself testified before the General Board of the Navy on January 23, 1942, that it was his considered opinion that "there would be a definite loss of efficiency in the Corps if we had to take Negroes."[2]

General Holcomb, in his concluding remarks before the Board, said,

> the Negro race has every opportunity now to satisfy its aspiration for combat, in the Army—a very much larger organization than the Navy or Marine Corps—and their desire to enter the naval service is largely, I think, to break into a club that does not want them.[3]

Regardless of all this opposition, the White House was insisting that the business of enlisting blacks for general duty in the Navy and Marine Corps must go forward. Wendell L. Wilkie, in a speech on 19 March, 1942, described the Navy's "racial bias" in excluding blacks from enlisting except as mess attendants as a "mockery." "Are we always as alert to practice (democracy) here at home as we are to proclaim it abroad?"[4]

The White House's answer, through Secretary of the Navy, Frank Knox, on 7 April was that the Navy, Coast Guard and Marine Corps would soon accept blacks for enlistment for general service in active duty reserve components. On 20 May the navy announced that on 1 June it would start recruiting 1,000 blacks a month and during June and July a complete battalion of 900 blacks would be formed by the Marine Corps.[5]

This is what one Marine officer recalled:

> . . . when the Colored came in we had the appropriations and the authority and we could have gotten 40,000 white people. It just scared us to death when the Colored were put on it. I went over to

Selective Service and saw General Hershey and he
turned me over to a lieutenant colonel (Campbell
C. Johnson)—that was in April—and he was one
grand person. I told him, "Eleanor (Mrs.
Roosevelt) says we gotta take in Negroes, and we
are just scared to death; we've never had any in; we
don't know how to handle them; we are afraid of
them."

He said, "I'll get the word around that if you want
to die young, join the Marines. So anybody that
joins (has) got to be pretty good!" And it was the
truth. We got some awfully good Negroes.[6]

To look into the possible uses of blacks in the Marine Corps
was the purpose of a study by Brigadier General Keller E. Rockey,
Director of Plans and Policies. It was first considered that perhaps
they could be used as mess men, as was being done in the Navy.
That was ruled out because the Corps did not have such a branch
at that time. No one believed that blacks could serve successfully
in combat units. After all, didn't the Army's General
Classification test scores show that the majority of black recruits
had low levels of aptitude? However it was inevitable that there
would be blacks in the Marines and at least some would serve in
combat units. A composite defense battalion containing antiaircraft artillery, seacoast artillery, infantry and tanks would be the
unit. Its task would be overseas base defense.

White units of this type were already deployed overseas and
seeing combat in such places as Wake and Midway Islands.

The officer chosen to head this black unit will be remembered
with admiration and respect by these first black Marines. He was
Colonel Samuel A. Woods, Jr. of South Carolina and a graduate
of The Citadel. He had twenty-five years experience as an officer,
including service in France in World War I, duty in Cuba, China,

the Dominican Republic and the Philippines and service with the fleet.[7] His personal qualities are what won him the almost universal admiration of the blacks. He was perceived by them to have a truly outstanding quality of absolute fairness. "He would throw the book at you if you had it coming, but he would certainly give you an opportunity to prove yourself."[8]

Colonel Woods lost no time in presenting his plan for action. By June 1, 1942, the first men to enlist were Alfred Masters and George O. Thompson, George W. James and John E. L. Tillman (2 June); Leonard L. Burns (3 June); and Edward A. Culp (5 June); all from the 8th Reserve District, headquartered at Pensacola, Florida. On 8 June, James W. Brown in the 3rd District (New York) and George L. Glover and David W. Sheppard in the 6th and 7th District (Charleston) enlisted.

Instructions to recruiters went out that the first men to be sent to Montford Point would be those who had skills that would help ready the camp for those to follow. Motivation to join the Marine Corps was high. Edgar R. Huff from Gadsden, Alabama who later became senior Sergeant Major in the Marine Corps, had this to say, "I wanted to be a Marine because I had always heard that the Marine Corps was the toughest outfit going and I felt that I was the toughest going and so I wanted to be a member of the best organization." Sometime in his eagerness to enlist, the recruit stretched the truth a bit. A prime example would be Obie Hall who eventually became the first man in the first squad in the first regular recruit platoon organized at Montford Point. He told the recruiting sergeant that he could drive a truck. He later recalled, "I could no more drive a truck than a man in the moon, [but] I said, 'I am a truck driver.' "[9] And as a result, he arrived at Montford on 2 September 1942.

Business Began

Recruit training began in September. The 1st, 2nd and 3rd recruit platoons were organized with forty men in each platoon. It was not long before exceptional recruits were being assigned as assistant to the Special Enlisted Staff (SES) as drill instructors. The camp consisted of:

> . . . A headquarters building (#100), a chapel, two warehouses, a theater building with two wings, which later housed a library, barber shop and classification room on one side and a recreation slop chute (beer hall) on the other, a dispensary building, a mess hall, designated by recruits as "The Greasy Spoon," quarters for the SES personnel, a small steam generating plant, a small motor transport compound, a small officer's club, and 120 green prefabricated huts each designed to house sixteen men.[10]

The camp site covered about 5 1/2 square miles with lots of mosquitoes and snakes around. Bears wandered about through the camp sometimes at night much to the dismay of the recruits who saw their tracks when they fell out for morning roll call.

With Colonel Woods as Battalion Commander, Headquarters and Service Battery (H&S) of the 51st Composite Defense Battalion was activated at Montford Point. Battery strength was 23 officers and 90 enlisted men—all white. The enlisted men would soon be known to the black recruits as SES men.

Gilbert H. Johnson, a recruit at the time and later to be known as "Hash Mark," recalled that discipline seemed to be these SES men's lone stock in trade and that they applied it with a vengeance, very much to our later benefit.[11]

26 August 1942, 13 of 24 black recruits expected arrived at Montford Point. The first black private to set foot in camp was Howard P. Perry of Charlotte, North Carolina. He was joined on that day by Jerome D. Alcorn, Willie B. Cameron, Otto Cherry, Lawrence S. Cooper, Harold O. Ector, Eddie Lee, Ulysses J. Lucas, Robert S. Parks, Jr., Edward Polin, Jr., Emerson E. Roberts, Gilbert C. Rousan and James O. Stallworth. The rest of the men scheduled to arrive in August came in over the next five days. Battery A of the 51st Composite Defense Battalion was organized on the 26th of August as an "Administrative and tactical unit for training recruit platoons."[12]

Hash Mark Johnson asked for and got a release from the Navy in order to joint the Marines. He was thirty-seven when he reached Montford Point with a serious dedication to becoming a good Marine. He was destined to succeed as an elder statesman and historian of the Montford Point Scenario.

Hash Mark Johnson was far from being the only unforgettable man who joined the ranks of those first volunteers in the Marine Corps. The recruiters had been very selective; there were others with prior military service: John T. Pridgen who had been a member of the black 10th Calvary in the late 1930s and George A. Jackson who had been an army lieutenant. Both soon became drill instructors. There were many college graduates and men who had some college training. Charles F. Anderson, a graduate of Morehouse College, who became the first black Sergeant Major of the Montford Point Camp and Charles W. Simmons, a graduate of Alcorn A&M with a Masters Degree from the University of Illinois, who eventually became Sergeant Major of the 51st Defense Battalion.[13] Sydney DesVigne and Raymond Floyd, both New Orleans educators with Masters degrees, and John D. Lewis of Raleigh, North Carolina would be among the memorable individuals entering the Corps with outstanding backgrounds.

By December 1942, the first boot camp graduates were offered a chance for a weeks furlough. Many went home for Christmas or New Year's Day. Many had unpleasant experiences because the existence of black Marines was not widely known yet. Some were stopped and questioned, some even arrested and detained for impersonating a Marine.

In January 1943, all men would be inducted into the service by the Selective Service System. The experience of a number of men entering at the top of the draft indicated that the promise by the draft board to continue to send the best available was being kept.[14] In May, Colonel Woods stated to the commandant that the standard of inductees continues to be about the same as in the case of volunteers. This indicates excellent work by the recruiting service.[15]

Change was beginning to take place during the first six months of 1943 at a rather fast pace. Hundreds of recruits began to come into Montford Point. New companies were formed, i.e., schools, motor transport, the 51st Rifle Company, the basis for organizing and dispatching depot companies (labor troops) to the field, also stewart cook schools were set up.

The most drastic change was on the recruit drill field. Most of the SES men had left by the end of April. There were now eight platoons in training. Black sergeants and corporals took over now as senior drill instructors: 16th—Edward R. Huff; 17th—Thomas Brokaw; 18th—Charles E. Allen; 19th—Gilbert H. Johnson; 20th—Arnold R. Bostic; 21st—Mortimer A. Cox; 22nd—Edward R. Davis; 23rd—George A. Jackson.[16] In late May, First Sergeant Robert W. Colwell, the last white drill instructor (SES man) was transferred and Sergeant Hashmark Johnson took his place as the recruit battalion's field sergeant major, in charge of all drill instructors. Sergeant Thomas Prigen was his assistant. From then on all recruit training at Montford Point was conducted by black NCO's—a milestone had been passed.

Boot Camp was not easier under Johnson, in fact, many say it was rougher. He had a reputation for being demanding but fair. He was determined that the black boots would measure up to Marine Corps standards.

While life was extremely tough for the "boots," it was not all drill and training.

The 51st was fortunate enough to have in its ranks, men from the bands of Duke Ellington, Erskine Hawkins, Cab Calloway and Count Basie, all members of the 51st band. There was always lots of music. Also the USO shows and movies and intramural sports between various units. There were several major league baseball players who would later participate in the World Series.

Topping all this was a young officer who arrived early at Montford Point by the name of Lieutenant Robert W. Troup, Jr., a composer and musician from New York. He was an immediate hit with everyone in camp. He became the recreation officer and many of his activities were directly responsible for the very high morale existing at the camp. It was not unusual to hear comments about Lt. Troup, such as: "A top-notch musician"; "A very decent sort of officer"; "He is the sharpest cat I ever seen in my life."[17]

While at Montford Point, Troup wrote a song, one Sunday afternoon, titled "Jacksonville." While the song was not meant to compete in any nation wide popular music chart, it will forever be a hit with certain Montford Point Marines. It went something like this:

> Take me away from Jacksonville, 'cause
> I've had my fill and that's no lie.
> Take me away from Jacksonville, keep me
> Away from Jacksonville until I die.
> Jacksonville stood still while the rest
> Of the world passed by.[18]

The popular "Jacksonville" was sung, whistled and remained high on the chart at Montford Point.

The 51st Defense Battalion

In April of 1943, Lieutenant Colonel Floyd A. Stephenson took over as Commanding Officer of the 51st. He had been at Pearl Harbor with the 4th Defense Battalion when the Japanese attacked.

In short order, within two weeks, he was recommending that the 51st become a regular heavy defense battalion. He stated, "there is nothing that suitable colored personnel can not be taught."[9]

Colonel Wood endorsed his recommendation. The recommendation was approved at Headquarters, Marine Corps on 28 May, 1943.

On 7 June, 1942, "Composite" was dropped from the title of the 51st. The 155mm Gun Battery expanded to become the 155mm Artillery Group and the Machine Group became the Special Weapons Group. The Rifle Company was now Company A, 7th Separate Infantry Battalion and the 75s became the 7th Separate Pack Howitzer Battery.

In July the changes continued. The 155mm became the Sea Coast Artillery Group and the 90s the Antiaircraft Artillery Group.[20]

The pace of the training was increased and unfortunately marred by the death on 20 August of the first black to die in Marine Corps uniform, Corporal Gilbert Fraser, Jr. of the 51st Seacoast Artillery Group.

Fraser, a New Yorker who had attended Virginia Union College, was killed when he fell thirty feet from a landing net into a landing boat while his unit was practicing debarkation. A road leading from the main camp at Montford Point to the base artillery area was named after the popular 30-year-old Marine. Lieutenant Colonel Stephenson noted that Fraser Road would be "a constant reminder to those who came after him of the fine type of young manhood represented by Gilbert Fraser."[21]

Throughout the fall of 1943, the training was tough. The whole battalion spent two months in the field. The Seacoast Group; the Antiaircraft and Special Weapons Group all testing their gunnery on Onslow Beach under very difficult weather conditions. While a number of officers noted in their December report that they thought the 51st needed more training—Secretary Knox and General Holcomb, on an inspection tour, watched the 90mm guns shoot down towed targets within sixty seconds and declared, "I think they [the 51st] are ready now."

In January 1944, the 51st was headed for San Diego and overseas duty.

The 51st boarded a merchant transport, SS Meteor at San Diego and sailed on February 11. The destination was the Ellice Islands. En route to the islands, on the 23rd of February, Detachment A was organized with Lieutenant Gould P. Groves as its commander. The new detachment would provide a garrison for Nanomea Island. The rest of the battalion was headed for Funafuti and would outpost Nukufetau.

In a landing ship (LST) with a submarine chaser for an escort, Detachment A arrived at Nanomea on 25 February 1944. The rest of the battalion disembarked at Funafuti on the 27th.[22]

Detachment A's mission was to maintain and defend the air fields on Nanomea and its outpost. On Funafuti, Colonel LeGette was charged with maintaining existing staging and limited repair facilities for aircraft, an anchorage and motor torpedo boat base, and with defending it all.

Nothing much happened to the 51st on its first overseas assignment, although the 155mm gun crews on Nanomea got off eleven rounds at a suspected enemy submarine on March 28.

A letter from the commandant in June arrived at Funafuti. The letter indicated that the 51st ordnance and motor transport equipment left behind in California showed signs of lack of proper preventive maintenance. This touched off somewhat of a disagreement between Colonel LeGette and Lieutenant Colonel Stephenson. Colonel LeGette ordered a board of investigation and appointed himself the examining officer.[23] The investigation was long and included testimony from battery and group commanders. It concluded that the former commanding officer was at fault.[24] Colonel LeGette followed up his investigation report with an unfavorable report the next month on the state of the 51st combat efficiency.

Meanwhile, Lieutenant Colonel Stephenson was engaged in a letter writing siege to Washington to tell his side of the story. Much of this correspondence forms the basis for what is known about the status of the 51st training and capabilities—at least from the stand point of the battalion officers. Throughout it all Stephenson maintained a strong defense of the 51st, the unit he had trained. He called it "the finest organization in the whole Negro Program in the Marine Corps . . ."[25] Much of this exchange went on without the knowledge of the men in the ranks of the 51st Defense Battalion. A glaring example of how personalities can cloud issues.

By July 1944 changes again began occurring in preparation to move to a more forward area. Eventually on September 8th the

51st sailed on an old Dutch-manned ship. The destination was Eniwetok Atoll in the Marshall Islands. The unit arrived at Eniwetok on September 14 where it replaced elements of the 10th antiaircraft battalion taking over its weapons and equipment on Eniwetok, Engebi Parry, and Porky Islands.

Talents as gunners were really sharpened at Eniwetok. The Battalion felt ready for anything, but the fact remained: no combat.

There was action for the 51st at Eniwetok, but nothing of substance. In February there was a week long submarine alert with many contacts, but no sightings. Later in the spring, Condition Red was sounded and the men ran hopefully to their positions, but no enemy planes appeared. Morale was pretty low. A former sergeant recalled "the routine got so boresome we got a few plane crashes, once in awhile, a ship would go down at sea trying to land, but other than that they were disappointed that they didn't actually get into combat. That was what they wanted!"[26]

Once the war was over, the men of the 51st, like everyone else, were anxious to get home.

On Thanksgiving day 22 November 1945, the main body of the 51st left Eniwetok for San Diego on a cargo ship, USS Sibik (AK–121).

The USS Sibik arrived at San Diego on 10 December and the battalion moved to Camp Pendleton, where those men who lived west of the Mississippi and had enough points were discharged. The discharging process continued for others at Camp Lejeune. On January 31, 1946, the 51st Defense Battalion was formally disbanded and the remaining low point men were transferred to other units at Montford Point.

It should be noted however, that several days before the departure of the main body of the 51st, a propped-up aircraft carrier, called the Sgt. Bay, was yanked out of moth balls to transport a contingent of men who were the first to qualify under the point system. They also began the discharging process at San Diego and continued at Camp Lejeune.

It would be a monumental mistake not to include the following excerpt in its entirety from the book mentioned above, *Blacks in the Marine Corps*:

> The first black Marine to complete thirty years of regular service retired on 28 September 1972. His military life spanned the dark years of segregation and gradual advance toward integration to the present climate of human awareness.
>
> When Sergeant Major Huff ended his active duty years, he summed up a varied and honored career with a simple oft repeated statement: "The Marine Corps has been good to me and I feel I have been good to the Marine Corps.[27]

There can be no better yardstick by which to evaluate the worth of the Corps to black Marines and their worth in return than that philosophy for good measure received, good measure given.

The grand old man in the history of black Marines would have to be Sergeant Major Gilbert H. "Hash Mark" Johnson. Tough as nails when he presided over the recruit drill field at Montford Point, and imbued throughout his career with a driving ambition for black Marines to succeed to be somebody, he mellowed somewhat in later life to the status of elder statesman and spokesman for a generation of men who led the way toward desegregation and the end of discrimination in the Marine Corps. He died, stricken by a heart attack, while addressing a testimonial dinner of the Camp Lejeune Chapter of the Montford Point Marine Association on August 5, 1972.

His topic, typically, was the history of the MPMA and blacks in the Marines.[28] There could have been no man prouder of the accomplishments of black Marines, and perhaps no man who left such a personal mark on others through his insistence that the first of his race in the Corps would "measure up." It was altogether fitting, therefore, that his name was commemorated in the Marine Corps where it first began to be known. On the recommendation of the Executive Board of the MPMA, endorsed by Assistant Secretary of the Navy, James E. Johnson, himself a Montford Pointer, the Commandant General Cushman, approved the renaming of Montford Point Camp.[29] On April 19th, 1974 in ceremonies at Camp Lejeune, Camp Gilbert H. Johnson was activated at Montford Point.[30] This well deserved tribute to a distinguished human being honors every black man and woman who has worn the Marine uniform, as he did, with pride of self and Corps.

Although the 51st Defense Battalion will be remembered as the Vanguard Unit in this historical beachhead, the 52nd and all subsequent units and individuals must be recognized as major players of notable significance in the overall picture.

In that regard, it would be unthinkable to not include and acknowledge the contributions made by the black Depot and Ammunition Companies during World War II.

Depot and Ammunition Companies

While the 51st Defense Battalion had been designated trained and publicized as a Combat Organization, one important fact was that it never saw combat. Instead, so called "labor troops," Marine depot and ammunition companies were the ones who received battle credits and suffered the lion's share of the casualties during World War II. During the early days of the war, quite a number of these brave and courageous men began their Marine Corps duty as members of the 51st Defense Battalion, later to be transferred into depot and ammunition companies.

One of the ironies of the service of these men was that their duties were not supposed to bring them into direct confrontation with the Japanese, yet the Personnel Department at Headquarters Marine Corps in one postwar tabulation of casualties established that nine black marines were killed in action or died of wounds while seventy-eight others were wounded in action and nine suffered from combat fatigue; thirty-five men died of other causes. All things considered, a significant casualty.

Overseas Service
Three weeks after its organization, the First Marine Depot

Company was on a train bound for San Diego, arriving April 5, 1943. On April 18, the company was on a ship bound for Novmea on New Caledonia. Movement of other depot companies to New Caledonia and the Solomons continued, to help support ongoing operations in the South and Southwest Pacific Theaters.

Saipan was the first target. The black depot and ammunition units helped load and unload the supplies of the assault forces, most of the black Marine units at Saipan got ashore on D–Day, June 15, 1944. This is what Sergeant Ernest W. Coney of the 3rd Marine Ammunition Company had to say about the landing:

> Sixteen men were assigned to the ships' platoons and twenty-five to floating dumps [pontoon barges moored just off the reef's edge as transfer points]. The rest got ready to disembark at 0700. At 0600 it was bright enough to see an island dead ahead and smoke was pouring up from the earth as our planes was bombing and strafing. . .
>
> We went over the side at 0700 and into the wait-ing landing boat. We shoved off toward the island and as usual we rode around in circles before going ashore. When we did start for the island, shells began to fall all around us. We was given orders to turn around and get into an amphibious alligator 'cause we could not make it in in the landing boat.
>
> We changed over and then waited. . . . we hit the beach at 1400 and immediately started diggin' in because it seemed as though the Japs had gotten the range. One team had an amphibian tractor shot out from under it as it was being unloaded— miraculously all the men escaped without injury.[31]

The Marianas

PFC Leroy Seals of Brooklyn, New York, was not so lucky. He was wounded a few hours after landing and died the next day. A mortar shell hit and exploded about twenty-five feet from a platoon that had just embarked with supplies and ammunition. It caused four casualties: PFC Charles F. Smith, Privates Albert W. Sims, Jeff Smith and Hayse Stewart. During the night of D–Day, the 18th Depot helped mop up a small enemy group that had managed to infiltrate the position between the 23rd and 8th Marines. After this was accomplished, the 18th was pulled out to resume its normal duties of handling supplies. This is what Captain William M. Barr reported of this period:

> Mortar shells were still raining down as my boys unloaded ammunition, demolition material, and other supplies from amphibious trucks. They set up "security" to keep out snipers as they helped load casualties aboard boats to go to hospital ships. Rifle fire was thick as they rode guard on trucks carrying high octane gasoline from the beach. A squad leader killed a Jap sniper that had crawled into a foxhole next to his. They stood waist deep in surf unloading boats as vital supplies of food and water were brought in . . . there were only a few scattered snipers on the beach. My boys accounted for several of these."[32]

Here is a brief account of D–Day experiences of the 20th Marine Depot Company given to the American Press by Captain William C. Adams.

> My company landed about 2 P.M. on D–Day [on Yellow Beach 2 supporting the 1st Battalion, 25th Marines]. We were the third wave, and all hell was breaking when we came in. It was still touch and

go when we hit shore and it took some time to establish a foothold.

My men performed excellently. I had previously told them: "You are the first Negro troops ever to go into action in the Marine Corps. What you do with the situation that confronts you, and how you perform, will be the basis on which you, and your race, will be judged. . . .

They did a swell job. . . . Among my own company casualties, my orderly was killed. My men are still living in foxholes."[33]

The orderly was Private Kenneth J. Tibbs of Columbus, Ohio, who died of wounds on D–Day. He was the first black Marine fatality as a result of enemy action in World War II. There were still other casualties in Negro companies on Saipan after the holocaust of D–Day. On June 16, Private Willie J. Atkinson of the 18th company was wounded and PFC Robert L. Neal of the Ammunition Company was shell shocked and hospitalized. PFC William B. Townsend of the 18th company was hit the next day. Second Lieutenant Edmund C. Forehand was wounded on the 21st and PFC Lawrence Dellerin, Jr. of the 20th company became a casualty the next day. As the fighting wore on in July, Corporal John S. Newsome of the 18th and Private Willie S. King of the 20th were wounded on the 4th; Private John S. Novy of the ammunition company was hit on the 9th and the last casualty of the battle, Private Willie Travis of the 18th was wounded on the 13th.

General Vandergrift, the commandant of the Marine Corps had this to say about the black Marines: "The Negro Marines are no longer on trial. They are Marines, period."[34]

Robert Sherrod, the war correspondent, reported in *Time*: "Negro Marines, under fire for the first time, have rated a universal

4.0 on Saipon."[35] In the Naval efficiency rating system there could be no higher mark.

The 3rd Ammunition and 18th, 19th and 20th Depot Companies were included in the Presidential Unit Citation awarded the 4th Marine Division for its combat role on Saipan and Tinian and Nealey island.

Combat on Peleliu

The 11th Marine Depot Company and the 7th Marine Ammunition Company "were destined to take part in the bloody battle for the island of Peleliu."

On September 15th, assault waves of the 1st Marine Division began landing on Peleliu in the face of heavy enemy fire. For the first few days, the black Marines unloaded supplies for the run on the beaches, but soon they began to work in dumps ashore moving supplies and ammo to the front lines.

The Japanese resistance was fierce and the black casualties mounted. The first black Marine wounded was Private Dyrel A. Shuler of the ammunition company, hit on the 20th of September. Two days later the 11th Depot had its first casualties, Private Predell Homblin. On the 23rd and 24th of September eight of the depot company Marines were wounded by enemy fire: Corporal Clifford W. Stewart; PFCs Willie A. Rushton, Carleton Shanks, JR., Kenneth R. Stevens; Edward J. Swain; Bernard L. Warfield; Earl L. Washington and Private Joseph Williams. Two days later, six more men were wounded: Corporal Lawrence B. Cale; PFCs Irving A. Banks; Timothy Black, Paul B. Cook, Oscar A. Edmonds, and Edgar T. Grace. In October, two more men of the 11th Depot Company were wounded, both on the 19th, Gunnery Sergeant Victor B. Kee and Private Everett Seals, giving the company the highest casualty rate of any black unit in World War II.

Fred deClouet

The 7th Ammunition suffered the last black Marine casualties on Peleliu: Corporal Charles E. Cain, wounded on October 9th and Private John Copeland died of wounds received the same day.

Major General William H. Rurpertus, commanding the 1st Division, wrote an identical letter of commendation to each of the Commanding Officers:

> 1. The performance of duty of the officers and men of your command has, throughout the landing on Peleliu and the assault phase, been such as to warrant the highest praise. Unit commanders have repeatedly brought to my attention the whole-hearted cooperation and untiring efforts exhibited by each individual.

> 2. The Negro race can be well proud of the work performed by the 7th Ammunition Company [11th Depot Company] as they have demonstrated in every respect that they appreciate the privilege of wearing a Marine uniform and serving with Marines in combat. Please convey to your command these sentiments and inform them that in the eyes of the entire division they have earned a "Well Done."[36]

The black Marines continued to perform on Iwo Jima and Okinawa as they had done previously, but not without cost. Many casualties were suffered. This is what Colonel Leland S. Swindler, Command of the 8th Field Depot had to say about a bloody battle on Iwo Jima one night with 200 to 300 Japanese—a battle in which the black Marines were in the thick of the fighting:

> ...highly gratified with the performance of these colored troops, whose normal function is that of labor troops, while in direct contact with the enemy for the first time. Proper security prevented

their being taken unaware, and they conducted themselves with marked coolness and courage. Careful investigation shows that they displayed modesty in reporting their own part in the action.[37]

This account of the black Marine Corps Depot and Ammunition Companies during World War II does not by any means, pretend to be exhaustive. Additional information is available by contacting the Director for Marine Corps History, Washington, D.C.

Anthology

SERGEANT MAJOR EDGAR R. HUFF
GADSDEN, ALABAMA AND HUBERT, NORTH CAROLINA

Portions excerpted from Bloods: An Oral History *by Wallace Terry. Copyright 1984–85, Random House Inc. Reprinted by Permission.*

We had a grand time. My retirement party on my two-and-one half-acre home here in Hubert, North Carolina, just down the road from Camp LeJeune. That was 1 October '72. We had some 750 people here on this lawn. All types of people. There was a twelve-piece orchestra on the lawn. We had all the barbecue pits going. Four hogs on the spit. My soul pot was in operation with chicken stew.

I heard they drank somewhere in the neighborhood of ten barrels of Tom Collins and martinis. The party was supposed to last from three o-clock until six. Apparently they forgot the time, because the last folks left the next morning. I never been to a ball like that in my life. I couldn't stand but one retirement, I'm sure.

When I retired, I had been sergeant major longer than anyone on duty at the time in all the services. I was the senior enlisted man in the whole United States Armed Forces. I could look back to becoming the first black sergeant major in the Marine Corps, serving nineteen different generals, and being sergeant major to General Cushman three times, including Vietnam, when it was the largest Marine force ever assembled. After I made sergeant major, it was twelve years before the Marines made another black one.

I guess I heard from two thirds of the generals on active duty at the time I retired, all the way to Okinawa and Japan. General Cushman called me his strong right arm, and President Nixon sent greetings. But Alabama was somethin'. They made me honorary mayor of my hometown, Gadsden, and gave me the key to the city. Governor Wallace sent his representative, the commander of the National Guard of the state of Alabama, and called to tell me how proud he was of my career and how it stands as an example for others to follow.

That's a long way to come for a boy who come into the Marines so poor he had just a quarter in his pocket, had pasteboard in his shoes to cover the holes, and one pair of drawers with a knot tied in the damn seat to keep them from flappin' around like a dress.

I was six when Daddy died, and it was just me and Mama. He was gassed while serving in Europe in World War II, and I think he never got over the effects. Mama made three dollars a week working for white folks, and I used to rake coke from the white people's ashes they threw away so we could get some heat in the fireplace. But when I got to be twelve, Mama wanted me to have a gun and learn how to shoot 'cause Daddy was a soldier boy. So she took in washing for fifty cents a week until she got enough money to buy this gun. It was a single barrel .22.

When I was fifteen, Mama got sick and needed an operation. So I dropped out of school—I guess it was the eighth grade—and went to work at Republic Steel. By 1942, I was making $1.40 a day and was the first black man to ever operate a overhead crane at the steel company. I was still walking four miles to work, too.

Well, one morning, this white man, Mr. Wilcox, who was going to relieve me, had this newspaper, and he showed me a story. "Ed," he said, "here's a new thing starting. If a Negro is qualified, he can join the Marines. That's the greatest outfit that's ever been. I was a Marine. If you join the Marines, you'll go places. It will take nothing but a lot of hard work, and you do what you're told."

I heard the Marines were the toughest outfit in the world, and I knew they couldn't be any tougher than what I was going through. So I decided to join.

Mama said, "Son, I don't want you to go into the service, but it was your father's wish. He wanted a soldier boy and a Red Cross girl."

So I walked down to the post office at 6th and Broad. But the Marine recruiter wasn't there. I asked the Army recruiter when he would be back. This Army sergeant said, "Ain't no niggers in the Marine Corps, but we got 'em in the Army. Come on. Let me sign you up." It was a common thing in those days for a white man to talk to you anyway he wanted to. He call you a nigger, it's like, "Hello James." "Hello, Ed."

It wasn't no big thing. And besides, I looked good to him. I was 6 foot 6, and 202 pounds.

I saw the Marie recruiter the next day, and he didn't talk like this Army sergeant. He said, "Boy, can you read?"

I said, "Yes, sir."

"What does that sign say?"

"Walk on in."

"Well, come on in."

Well, I passed the written test, but I needed $1.80 to get the bus to Birmingham and back for the physical examination. I had

27

seven cents. Mama had thirteen cents. Well, Mr. Wilcox loaned me $2, which I paid him back on my first payday in the Marine Corps.

They notified me on June 26, 1942, that I was going into the Marine Corps. One of the first fifty blacks to get accepted.

In September I got my papers, my orders and train tickets to report to duty in North Carolina. I put on my big apple hat, my triple-E shoes, peg pants, and zoot suit. And went down to the railhead. It was the first time I ever left home. Of course, I had never been on a train in my life.

When I got to North Carolina, I felt like a foreigner. It was the first time I ever talked to anybody that wasn't from Alabama.

We got trained at Montford Point, next to Camp Lejeune. We had a completely Negro Marine Corps. We had out own barracks, our own infantry, our own tanks, our own guns. It couldn't have been more segregated. Of course, the officers was white.

When I went to bed the first night, I heard this music. I started crying, wondering what my mama was doing. So I asked this boy, why in the world is they playing that song. They told me that was taps. I had never heard a bugle before in my life. I swear 'fore God.

When I went to dinner the next day, I tried a little piece of this ham. It was the toughest ham I ever ate in my life. So I wrote to Mama to send me some pieces of ham out the smokehouse. Later on, they put that ham out there again, and this friend of mine said, "Ed, that ain't no ham."

I said, "The hell it ain't."

"That's corned beef."

And that's the first I ever knew they had corned beef.

In December I had just finished boot camp when Colonel Woods called me in. "Got a telegram. Your mother is real sick. They want you to come home. At once." See, I don't have a brother or sister or nobody. Just my mother and myself. And I said, "I can't. I don't have no money to go home." We wasn't getting but thirty dollars a month, and I had me an allotment out to my other.

He said, "I tell you what. I am going to give you fifteen dollars so you can go home to see your mama."

I said, "Yes, sir." You don't ask him no question. You do what the hell you told. And he gave me a furlough.

So I got on the bus, and when it pulled into Atlanta, I got off and went in the station. It was two Marine MPs. They walked up to me. One said, "Hey, boy, C'mere."

I started out with my little bag.

"What you doing with that uniform on?"

I say, "I'm a Marine."

They say, "There ain't no damn nigger Marines. You going to jail."

I give them my furlough papers. They tore 'em up right in my damn face. Said I was impersonating a Marine.

They started to turn me loose. Say, "You go in there and pull that damn uniform off. You ain't got no clothes to wear, yo go to the relief."

I say, "I'm not impersonating a Marine. I am a Marine."

"You going to get it."

They took me down to the city jail and had me locked up. That night a Marine captain came in to get some white Marines who've been locked up for bein' drunk. I knew a captain when I see a captain, so I ask him to get me out, too.

"Ain't no nigger Marines. We heard about you."

I was there the twenty-third, the twenty-fourth. And they took us out to pick up trash and garbage. And there I was in jail on my first Christmas in the Marine Corps.

When the Navy chaplain came in for Christmas prayers, he wouldn't even talk to me.

Finally, a Marine major came in. It must have been the twenty-eighth. And I convinced him to call Colonel Woods, even though he thought I was making up a bunch of lies. He didn't know about Montford Point, being as it was a brand new camp.

Colonel Woods told the major to get me out now, and he told me to go home and don't worry about any papers.

Colonel Woods is dead now. But I got his picture. Colonel Samuel S. Wood Jr. The first commanding officer ever commanding black Marines.

General Larsen was somethin' else. He was the commanding general of Camp Lejeune. One day he came over to speak to us at this smoker. No Negro was allowed to be on LeJuene unless he was accompanied by a white Marine to go to a specific place with a chit stating what he was going to do there. I'll never forget when he walked in. It was the first general we had ever seen. Here I am, a hard charger, thinking I want to be a general. I want to be like him.

Well he started talking about the war. He said, "I just came back from Guadalcanal. I've been fighting through the jungles. Fighting day and night. But I didn't realize there was a war going on until I came back to the United States. And especially tonight. When I come back and I find out that we have now got women Marines, we have got dog Marines, and when I see you people wearing our uniforms, then I know there's a war going on."

Goddamn. You never saw so many Coke bottles fly. Knocked him down. And there was a riot that night. The first black riot in Marine Corps history.

Well, I went from private to first sergeant in just twenty-three months and became the sergeant in charge of training all the black Marines. When we shipped out to the Pacific, we moved supplies to the fighting units that were all white. After that, I took the first black unit into Tsien Tsin, the first to step on Chinese soil. In Korea I fought in a weapons company, which of course, was integrated by then. But over the years, I was so unhappy sometimes in the Marine Corps, I didn't know what to do. If there's ever a man should be prejudiced as far as the white man is concerned, I should be. 'Cause some of these officers kicked me every way but loose.

Back in '57, when I was sergeant major right here in Camp Lejeune, the executive officer of headquarters battalion got half drunk and called me into his office.

He say, "C'mere, boy."

I've been called boy so many times you automatically move like a robot even knowing you wasn't a boy.

He said, "How 'bout a drink?"

"No, sir. I don't drink during working hours."

"You think you too good to drink with me?"

He shoved the bottle in my face. And when he did that, I turned right around and walked right out. If I had hit him, I would have been in the penitentiary for striking any officer.

Another time I was in a general's office, and he was talking on the phone. He says, "Now, colonel. The problem is not how many watermelons you have. It's how many niggers you got to eat 'em."

After he hung up, he look at me, and he said, "I'm sorry."

I say, "What did the general say?" When a general is on the phone, I don't know what he says. "You don't owe me no apology."

He said, "Ed, I'm telling you, ain't but one of your kind. Thank you very much."

And the sergeants could get to you, too. But by me being sergeant major they had to watch their step with me. reporting in and he telephone my quarters. This was 1963.

"Did you know what the damn chief clerk of yours done this evening?"

"No. What did he do?"

31

"He assigned me to stay in a room with a damn nigger."

I says, "Is that right?"

"Yes, sir, Sergeant Major. And I'd rather sleep on the parade ground under a flagpole than to sleep with a goddamn black nigger."

So, I says, "Well, I can take care of you tonight. Tomorrow, I'll assign you to your permanent quarters. I make it a practice to do everything I can especially for my staff NCOs."

So I arranged for this gunny to have the VIP quarters that night in the staff NCO club.

The next morning I told my driver to go down to supply and draw out a half a tent, five tent pegs, and one pole. I said, "You know one Marine don't rate but half a tent."

So I'm sitting there in my office with about twenty-five yards of campaign ribbons, a bucket of battle stars, and each one of my sleeves look like a zebra. Ain't no way in hell a man could not know I was not the sergeant major.

When the gunny walked in, he stopped and looked at me as though he saw a ghost.

He said, "Are you the sergeant major?"

I said, "Well, Gunny, you are familiar with the rank structure, aren't you?"

He said, "You not the one I talked to last night, are you?"

"Why sure I am. Sit down."

I made him drink some coffee, and the cup was rattlin' like it was a rattlesnake. Then I drove him out to the parade grounds up to the flagpole, and said, "Here is your quarters. Now you pitch your lean-to on the flagpole like you requested." And it was raining like hell.

When I came back, the tent was running full of water. I said, "Get this tent trenched out like it's supposed to be. You are ruining government property."

Then he said, "I'll stay with that fella."

I told him he would have to get this black sergeant to agree and bring him to my office. Well, it was all right with the sergeant, and the gunny moved in.

In about three weeks, I went down to the club and this black sergeant had a white woman, and the gunny had a black woman. Having the best time you ever saw. And a few months later, the gunny and the black woman was married. They live up here near me now and got two children. Doing real fine.

But I never let any of these things make me prejudiced right back. Especially in combat. Especially in Vietnam. I am the sergeant major. I take care of all my men, black and white.

Now when the Tet Offensive broke out in January of 1968, I was sergeant major of the 1st Military Police Battalion in Danang. At the time, our headquarters was right across from the main airstrip. Well, the rebels was trying to get to the headquarters of this Vietnamese general. And they made a break through down on River Road. So we had this blocking force right between the general's headquarters and the rebels.

The colonel and I was in a bunker at the time. The fighting was going on for about an hour, and we figured everything was going pretty smooth 'cause we had radio contact and everything. Then Kenny called in. He said, "Send help! Send help!"

I thought to myself, that's not the way Kenny calls.

And the colonel said, "What the hell's wrong out there?"

Kenny said, "The whole area's moving. The whole area's moving. Send help! Send help! They got us surrounded." Then he said, "Help! This is my last transmission."

And it was just like a breath was rolling out. And that was his last transmission.

And I told the colonel, "Let's go."

At that time I carried a shotgun, a pistol, and a grenade launcher. And two bandoliers also.

33

And when we got to the scene, you never saw a fire fight more horrifying in all your life. The boys were in a spot as hard as it could be, but they was holding it.

And I looked up, and the best radio operator you ever saw—name was Rick—was hit and pinned down out there maybe fifty yards. They saw him out there in this field, and they were trying to finish him off. They was shooting with automatic fire, you know. And every time Rick'd move a little, they would fire out after him. Just tryin' to finish him off.

Rick was hollering, "Mother. Mother."

I could stand it no more. I started out. And the colonel said, "No. No. Just wait. Just wait."

I said, "Sorry, Colonel."

This wasn't a black boy. He was a white boy. I knew I might get killed saving a white boy. But he was my man. That's what mattered.

And I took off. Ran through an open field. They was firing from a tree line. And I got maybe twenty yards, and I was hit in the head. It hit my helmet. And it spin me around, knocked me down. And I got up and started again. And another round hit on the side of the helmet and knocked me down again. And I started crawling. And it seemed like round after round was kicking at the dirt all around me.

And I jumped up then, and I started running. Then I got to him. Then they opened up everything they had right there into that position. And I fell on top of him to keep him from getting hit again, and this fragmentation grenade hit us and ripped my flack jacket all into pieces. And it got me in the shoulder and arm.

Then our people opened up all they had. And the Cong started moving back. And the colonel came out to help me with the stretcher to bring Rick back.

And then I went back and found Kenny. Kenny was killed. He was still holding the transmitter in his hand.

Then they tried to get me to go to the hospital, but, hell, I wasn't going to no damn hospital then, because my men was still scattered around and I had to get 'em together.

Well, I got pieces of steel still in me. And my wife still digs them out when they start coming up to the skin.

They gave me the Bronze Star for pullin' Rick out. And Rick wrote me this letter. It says, "Sergeant Major, I thank you for my life."

Hell, he was one of my men. Black or white, I would have done the same even if I got shot to hell in the process. And I was forty-eight at the time. And that boy couldn't have been much over twenty-one.

When I had my retirement party, I kinda wished that boy could've been there. Wouldn't that have been nice?

Well, sir, about three weeks after that party, we were having some friends over for dinner, and we were out on the patio. Sergeant Major Washington—he's a black sergeant major—and his wife were there, and another black lady. She was teaching at the Marine base. My son and some more kids were playing in the yard. It was just about dusk hour.

At this time, a car drove up. And four white Marines started throwing hand grenades. They were white phosphorous. Threw one right through my station wagon. Threw another at this lady's Cadillac. Guess they thought this was my Cadillac. And they threw another one into the house. And another one hit the Marine emblem on my gate. And everything was lit up like Christmas around here.

A white friend of mine saw them, and he took off at a high speed, and he did get that tag number. And some of the state troopers came out here and helped me put some of the fire out.

The Marine Corps never did nothin' to them at all. Three of them got transferred or discharged, although they were supposed to be held pending an investigation. Being a sergeant major in the goddamn Marine Corps for seventeen years, I know damn well that when a person is awaiting disciplinary action, he can't be transferred, discharged, or do a damn thing. I got pissed off. I've fought for thirty years for the Marine Corps. And I feel like I own part of this ground that I walk on everyday, especially this that is mine. So I went to the Naval investigator, and he said a report was turned over to the commanding officer. He said he talked to these guys who were trying to destroy my family and myself. He said they told him they didn't understand how a nigger could be living this way, sitting out there eating on a nice lawn, under that American flag I fly everyday.

I went to the deputy sheriff, an old buddy of mine, and he got hold of the boy who was still on the base. He told the boy I didn't want him to serve no jail time, I just wanted him to pay the damage he did. The boy's daddy telephoned me from Tennessee about he didn't have no money. I ain't never heard a white man beg to any black man like that in all the days of my life. A Southern white man. Well, he paid it.

You know, when they threw those grenades at my family, my friends, and my home, I thought back to the time the Ku Kluxers came and took Mr. Sam Brewster away. I was nine or ten at the time.

We heard all these cars blowin' horns. My grandfather said, "The Ku Klux is comin'."

My grandfather had a pistol. If the Ku Klux had known he had a pistol, they would have pitched camp at our house till they found it. Grandma and Granddad kept it in the top drawer of the chifforobe. He went and got that .44, turned out the lights, and looked out the door to see what would happen. The rest of us jumped under the bed and waited to see whose house they gon' bust into and who they gon' take away and beat up.

Mr. Sam Brewster lived four doors away. There was a lot of hollering and screaming going on. We heard a shot. And he was dragged out. They took him up to Lookout Mountain. Tied him to a tree. Took a whip, and beat that man like you never seen the like before. They thought he was dead. But he got loose and came back and laid down on the font porch of my grandfather's house.

I don't know for sure why they did it. But I think it had something to do with the store owner across the street—this white man—and Mr. Sam Brewster's wife. She was a real high yellow type. In fact, her family looked white. You couldn't tell the difference to save your life. The store owner wanted Mr. Sam Brewster's wife, and in those times you weren't suppose to do nothin' about it. But Mr. Sam Brewster was a big strong type, and he wouldn't have it.

The next day the store owner's arm was bandaged. That's how we knew he was Ku Kluxer. And that evening, they burned his store down—the Negro people did.

Whenever the Ku Kluxers would come, I would be terrified. It was the damnedest thing. And I thought about that many times when I was overseas, and I had those beautiful machine guns. I would just wish to hell I had somethin' like that back in Alabama when those sonofabitches came through there. I would have laid them out like I did those damn Congs. The same way.

I just don't see how black people survived down there in those days. I just don't see it.

STAFF SERGEANT RAYMOND B. FLOYD
NEW ORLEANS, LOUISIANA

RADAR TECHNICIAN
MONTFORD POINT, CAMP LEJEUNE
51ST DEFENSE BATTALION
1942–1945

It was in the month of June, 1942 when I raised my right hand and swore to defend my country within the ranks of a unit of the United States Military Force which until that time did not want or allow me or any of my race to be a part of its illustrious history of distinguished military action. Had it not been for the feelings and efforts of a few propitious, real Americans and some damaging propaganda by our enemy, Germany, my hand may never have had the opportunity to ascend for that cause.

Raymond Bertrand Floyd, son of George and Eva Floyd, graduated from Xavier University with a B.A. degree in Education, was employed at Xavier University Preparatory School and had received the Masters Degree in Education with a minor in Guidance. I had reported to a call from the Draft Board but received a six month deferment due to my teacher status. I was questioned by friends and associates as to why I was determined to give up this status and volunteer for the United States Marines. My answer then was the same as it would be now under the same conditions—I wanted to be an officer in the Marines. I had always wanted to be somebody among those whom I considered the best. I never let it bother me as to how difficult it might be to accomplish my aspiration. Nor did it ever come into my thinking that there were those within the Corps who were determine that such would never happen.

Upon arrival at Montford Point, my first disillusion came along with the sight of the makeshift base where we were to spend

38

months preparing to fight an enemy but being accepted as almost an enemy ourselves. But we were men, some of the best that America had to offer. We were black men and had been treated as if we were not wanted before and we had made it—we would make it this time—and we did with the help of the Almighty.

Following a never-to-be-forgotten three months of Boot Camp, I was requested to teach a "review" class in mathematics and bring those involved from Arithmetic through Logarithm in two weeks. This same group of thirty-six men was assigned to study radar for the next six months. As the class proceeded, six of us were selected to become technicians and the remaining group would serve as operators in six sections, each with a 268B Radar set consisting of three oversized trucks and a trailer. All groups were assigned to the 51st Defense Battalion and we departed the United States in this fashion.

Much has been told about the distinguished 51st in this book to the extent that I only wish to relate an accomplishment of our group never mentioned here or elsewhere in what has been recorded about our Battalion.

The 51st was the defensive unit on Eniwetok. The Japanese military wanted to determine how much fire power remained on the rear of our positions. Small Japanese submarines were detailed to get this information. We were informed of this situation. All radar units were ordered to track at zero degrees elevation in an attempt to detect this action by the enemy. The operators on my unit reported a "pip" at about 600 yards from shore where it was 900 feet deep. We stayed on this target for more than an hour with repeated reports to the battle line officer. Other radar sets picked up the target and reported. The 155 millimeter groups, our big guns, were fed the data. When all groups reported on target the command magnitude was seen and heard by all. We no longer had a pip on the scopes and the sub had been demolished.

39

Shortly after the activity described above an order came from Fleet Marine Force to most units in the South Pacific to send qualified Marines, one per unit, back to the States for Officer Candidate Ballition training.

It was not known at this time exactly how long the war would continue and the invasion of Japan was quite a possibility. The new classes were to be conducted at Hadnot Point of Camp LeJune, July 1, 1945. I was selected and I accepted without the least hesitation.

Within forty-eight hours I was on a plane headed to my first stop, Hawaii. Upon arrival at Fleet Marine Force Headquarters in Hawaii, I was informed that my orders had to be changed to the second class which would begin on 1 August 1945. I did not mind this because I would have more time in Hawaii, travel by boat to the U.S. and have more time at home.

I arrived at midnight at Camp Hadnot Point. The Officer of the Day viewed my orders and said I would be sent to Montford Point to await the opening of the class a week later. Arriving at Montford Point, I discovered that there were two other Black Marines waiting to go to OCB on 1 August.

Three Black Marines worked a full day every day preparing to enter the class on the prescribed date. We field-stripped weapons, read manuals, and ran track, and quizzed each other day and night. Each day we checked Headquarters to determine if our orders (to go eight miles to Hadnot Point) had arrived. Each time the answer was negative.

Came 1 August 1945 and our orders had still not arrived. 2 August, 3 August followed and no orders. How did we feel? It would be too hard to accurately describe. I had come 8000 miles to attend a OCB class and now eight miles away I was not permitted to attend. Why? Because I was Black. I secured a pass and went to New York to relieve the stress. I came back, no orders; I went back to New York. Upon returning this time, after two bombs had been dropped upon Japan, I was told that the three of us should go to Hadnot Point for further orders. The war was over for all practical purposes and the OCB class (which had started) had been terminated.

The three black "would have been candidates" went to Hadnot Point feeling like anything else but Marines. We were given four options:

1. Go back to your former outfit oversees

2. Apply for peacetime OCB (they would never allow this)

3. Apply for Reserve Officer Training for six weeks with a guarantee of being commissioned upon completion of the prescribed period.

4. Accept discharge.

But there was a requirement which the Marine Corps knew would keep a Black Marine from being eligible for No. 3. All such candidates must have had a completed V-12 Program before entering the Marines. But wait, PFC Frederick Branch had gone to Purdue before entering the Marines, had taken V-12 and was therefore eligible for training and commissioning. He would be the first black officer in the United States Marines. None of the top brass expected that this would happen. The other two of us were as happy as if it actually applied to us. The Corps had made certain that a Black would not become an officer and now it was within reach. However, PFC Branch had just married and did not wish to be away from his new bride as long as it would take.

This was an internal situation which required the cooperation of all of us at Montford Point. We had to get PFC Branch to reconsider.

To accomplish this we regrettably, but deliberately, avoided him at every occasion—on duty, at leisure, off base, "Slop Shoot" drinking beer, everywhere. Five days later at Hadnot Point he applied for Reserve Officer Training and everybody was happy at Montford Point.

He became the first black officer in the U.S. Marine Corps in November 1945.

I accepted discharge and applied for employment in Veterans Administration. The first four of our race were employed in this government operation in 1946. At the same time I applied for a commission in the U.S. Army Reserve and received such as a Captain. I had reached the rank of Lt. Colonel before retirement.

Upon leaving the V.A. after four plus years, I was employed at Xavier University. While there I worked on my terminal degree and received such in 1959 from Columbia University in New York. During this entire period I organized and led Civil Rights groups in New Orleans and was very successful in this effort (a long story in itself).

I resigned from Xavier and went to Fort Valley for three years. In 1963 I returned to Louisiana as a full professor and head of the Department of Counselor Education at Southern University in Baton Rouge, La. and I am there now. Retirement? I am still too young for such.

CAPTAIN ROBERT (BOBBY) TROOP
ENCINO, CALIFORNIA

RECREATION OFFICER, MONTFORD POINT CAMP
51ST DEFENSE BATTALION
COMMANDING OFFICER, 6TH MARINE DEPOT COMPANY
U. S. MARINE CORPS
1942–1946

I was one of the twelve original officers to see the first black marines in June, 1942 at Montford Point Camp in Jacksonville, North Carolina. The camp or area surrounding Montford Point was vast and was known as New River, later becoming Camp LeJeune. Up to June of 1942 there had never been a black marine.

The Marine Corps almost proudly called itself "the exclusive branch" of the service. The Army, Navy and Air Corps had blacks, but not the Marine Corps. Then it was generally observed that through pressure from Eleanor Roosevelt and Harry Hopkins, Montford Point Camp came into being as a training base for Defense Battalions for exclusively black enlisted personnel and white officers.

I volunteered for this duty as an officer and I never regretted it. I liked the men, their spirit, sense of humor and dedication. They looked like they were so proud to be Marines and they were.

I think some of the other officers were not that keen about my closeness to the troops, nor were they that enthusiastic about my defending the ten or twenty involved in General Court Martials at Hadnot Point. I have to confess that I really did not care.

I believe Colonel Samuel Woods was an excellent choice for the commanding officer of Montford Point Camp. No one could have handled the sensitive and sometimes precarious situation more ably or understandingly. The men respected him and looked up to him and they should have.

As Recreation Officer and with immeasurable help from Lt. Richard Goodwin; Hiney Thomas, prize fighter; Dan Bankhead, Major league pitcher; Finis Henderson, dancer/singer and Master Sgt. Joe Wilder, I saw Montford Point emerge with remarkable football, baseball and boxing teams. It had possibly the most professional dance orchestra and marching band in all of Camp Lejeune. Montford Point presented a very well received musical show at the very impressive (and huge) Hadnot Point Theater.

I served at Montford Point until December 1944 at which time I became the Commanding Officer of the Sixth Marine Depot Company assigned to duty on Saipan attached to the Second Marine Division.

I do not believe the black Marines were given an opportunity to prove themselves as Marines in World War II. They were given little or no chance in combat. There was complete segregation. They became box and ammunition carriers. There were no black officers.

I remember recommending a Sgt. Powell who had graduated from college with honors and was considered for All-American selection in football for Officer's Training. He was refused admission for "Medical reasons." I also recommended others with equally good credentials. They too were turned down. I was proud of the black Marines on Saipan. For the most part they served admirably and well. They can look back on it with pride.

But I am remembering things that happened nearly fifty years ago. Those things have certainly changed. Today we have integration and black officers. Its a vastly different Marine Corps and I couldn't be happier.

GUNNERY SERGEANT ARNOLD R. BOSTIC
MONTCLAIR, NEW JERSEY

155 NM SEACOAST BATTERY COMMANDER
MILITARY PROVOST SERGEANT
MONTFORD POINT CAMP LEJEUNE
51ST DEFENSE BATTALION
1942–1945

I enlisted in the Marine Corps for two reasons: (1) to avoid being drafted into the Army or Navy. (2) I wanted to become a member of the toughest branch of the service and was willing to accept the challenges to succeed in that branch. I had no idea at the time due to my being only eighteen years old, that the challenges I was to face would play such an important part not only in my life but in the future status of black Marines in the Marine Corps. I was called to active duty on July 29, 1942.

Upon boarding the train in Newark, N.J. to proceed to Montford Point, Camp Lejeune, New River, North Carolina, I met another black Marine, one Charles Gray from Buffalo, New York, who was also ordered to report to Montford Point. After an uneventful trip from Newark, N.J., we left the train at Rocky Mount, North Carolina to board a bus for Jacksonville, North Carolina. Prior to boarding the bus and having government issued meal tickets, we entered a restaurant which was located in a hotel opposite the train station. Upon being approached by a white waitress, I asked whether she accepted government meal tickets. She replied she did but we could not eat in the restaurant and we would have to go around back and receive our meal through an opening in the back door. We both ordered tremendous meals and told the waitress we would be in the back in twenty minutes. Upon exiting the front door, we ran down the hotel stairs, entered

45

a taxi with a black driver who stated he had observed us enter the hotel restaurant and knew we would not be served. The cab driver drove us across the railroad tracks where we had a sumptuous meal. We both gave the black owner six unused meal tickets. Gray nor I had never been south of the Mason-Dixon Line before, so after that experience we both knew where we were. (Challenge #1 the System.)

Upon arriving at the Jacksonville, N.C. bus station, we were met by a short white Marine Corporal who after asking us whether we were reporting for duty at Montford Point and reading our orders, he pointed to a small green pickup truck and asked us did we see it. We both replied yes. He then yelled, "What the hell do you mean yes! From now on you will answer yes sir and no sir! Now on the double get in the truck!" We both asked what "on the double" meant. He told us both to turn around and he kicked us both in the ass and replied, "On the double means run!" After that experience, Gray and I never forgot what on the double meant. (Challenge #2.)

We arrived at Montford Point on August 2, 1942. There were approximately five or six black Marines at the base at that time. I was assigned to the first platoon. My Drill Instructors were Gunnery Sgt. Colwell and Corporal Comstock and Sgt. Nelson.

After completing boot camp in November 1942, I was promoted to PFC along with Johnson, Allen, Cox, Woods, Jackson. We were the first black Marine Drill Instructors. After bringing two platoons through boot camp, I was transferred to the 51st Defense Battalion in 1943. I was promoted to Corporal and Sergeant in 1943 and Platoon and Gunnery Sergeant in 1944. I left with the 51st Defense Battalion as 155mm Seacoast Battery Commander in February, 1944, and arrived in the Ellice Islands (Funafuti) in March. The 51st Defense Battalion was reassigned to the Marshall Islands in 1945. My Battery was assigned to

Eniwetok and after several months, I was transferred from coast artillery and commanded the Military Police Company as Provost Sergeant. After the war was over, the 51st Defense Battalion returned to the states in December 1945. I was honorable discharged in December 1945 at Montford Point with the rank of Gunnery Sergeant. After being discharged, I enlisted in the Marine Corps Reserves and after serving five years, was honorably discharged with the rank of Tech. Sergeant. Total service time: 8 years 6 months.

After discharge, I became a carpet and linoleum mechanic until after several years I developed water on my knees. I then became a police officer with the Montclair, New Jersey, police department in 1955 and retired with the rank of Lieutenant in 1982 after twenty-eight years of service. I now reside in Port Charlotte, Florida.

I shall never forget the first meeting of the New York Chapter of the Montford Point Marine Association (MPMA) which was held at one of the member's house in Jamaica in the 1950s. Jim Pettiford and I came over from Jersey. My wife gave me hell because I was out so late. I joined the MPMA not only because I am one of the original Montford Point Marine, but I believe in the goals and achievements that the MPMA is striving for. MPMA is part of Marine history.

As I now look back and remember the insults, racial remarks, abuses both mental and physical, that we original Montford Pointers endured, I am sure we all had the same silent determination that irregardless of our color we were Marines. I thank God I am still here and able to write this profile. Was it worth it? You damn better believe it was! After meeting and speaking with General Peterson both in Houston and St. Louis and seeing Black Marine Majors, Captains, Lieutenants in various cities during my

47

travels, I can't help but feel proud and think to myself, Arnold, you had a small part in their lives.

Semper Fidelis.
Arnold R. Bostic
Serial # 415940

Sergeant Gene Doughty
New York, New York

Squad Leader, First Platoon
36 Marine Depot Company
8th Field Service Regiment
Temporarily Attached to the
5th Marine Division
Montford Point Camp Lejeune
1942–1946

While Gene in his unassuming way and for reasons best known to himself, did not submit to an interview, it would be unthinkable not to provide a highlighted profile of this distinguished ex-Marine. Gene Doughty born in the city of Stanford, Connecticut., 3 March 1924. Family relocated to New York City in 1928. Completed primary education at PS 184, James Fenimore Jr., H.S. and Commerce H.S. in New York City. Enrolled at CCNY pursuing Physical and Health Education.

Gene was inducted into U.S. Marine Corps, April 16, 1943 at NYC Recruiting Station, along with fellow Montford Pointers Jimmy Sperling and Harold Knowles arrived at Montford Point Camp and began recruit training with 48th Platoon (Unit of First Black Marine Officer, Frederick C. Branch). Completed recruit training with 66th Platoon, after one month hospitalization at U.S. Naval Hospital, Hadnot Point.

He was assigned to Schools Co., Headquarters Bn. Satisfactorily completed Payroll/Muster Roll and Clerical courses. Promoted to Private First Class.

Private Doughty was promoted to Corporal in 1944. Assigned to 36th Marine Depot Co., classified as Field Squad Leader, 1st Squad, 1st Platoon (then 20 years of age). In November 1944 left

49

Norfolk, VA. aboard USS Bayfield. Final destination—Pearl Harbor, Oahu, Territory of Hawaii. Unit was attached to 8th Field Depot, 8th Service Regiment, 5th Marine Division along with 33rd, 34th Depot Companies and 8th Ammo Company. Advanced training conducted, period of eight weeks at Camp Catlin, Oahu.

Early February 1945, he departed from Oahu aboard LST 943, fully equipped for combatant area; destination unknown. Arrived at Iwo Jima, Volcanoe Islands on February 19th, 1945. Spent total of thirty-two days following initial landings. 36th Depot Co., along with other units were cited with Navy Unit Commendation.

Doughty departed for Hilo, Hawaii for rehabilitation and advanced training, preparatory for onslaught of Japanese mainland.

He was then promoted to Sergeant (Field Warrant) in May 1945. Assigned temporarily as Platoon Sergeant of First Platoon (then age 21).

Sergeant Doughty participated in armed occupation of Sasebo, southern island off Kyushu, Japan in late November 1945. Six months tour of duty. Departed for Guam, Marianas Islands; after brief stay was ordered to Treasure Island, Bay Area, California. Within a weeks time he departed for Montford Point Camp and was Honorably Discharged in May of 1946.

Shortly after arriving in NYC, he resumed secondary education. Was conferred with B.A. in Physical and Health Education at CCNY in 1948. Practical training included stints as Physical Ed. Instructor with Juvenile Aid Bureau, Police Athletic League, NYC Police Department and Assistant in Athletic Department of Catholic Youth Organization.

Between 1948 and 1954 Mr. Doughty was employed as Social Investigator, NYC Department of Welfare.

Between 1954 and 1969 he was employed as Sales, Service and later Store Manager of VIM ELECTRIC CO.

Between 1970 and 1985 Gene was employed at Sears, Roebuck and Company as Customer Service Manager. Later promoted to Department Manager of Floor Covering, Catalogue Sales, Home Improvement. Promoted to Division/Department Manager of Communication sales. He retired in May, 1985.

He is currently serving in voluntary roles, conduction and lecturing in Alcoholic and Drug Abuse groups (Co-dependents only—Serving on Board of Directors. Marine Corps Scholarship Foundation, Princeton, N.J. (three terms).

Montford Point Marine Association, Inc. Achievements: Two terms as President of N.Y. Metro Chapter. Six Years as National Vice-President, MPMA, Inc. Served two separate tenures as elected National President of MPMA, Inc. Currently serving as National Advisory Council Chairman, MPMA. Recipient of The Hashmark Johnson and Semper Fidelis Awards. Life Member— Marine Corps League.

MARINE CORPS VETERAN OF WORLD WAR II,
THE KOREAN AND VIETNAM WARS

We were on our way to Philadelphia International Airport to pick up Hari Rhodes, a Marine Corps veteran, who was currently starring in a prime-time TV series, "Daktari." Rhodes' novel about the first Black Marines had been published by Bantam Books in January, 1965. He was to be a featured speaker at the First National Reunion of Montford Point Marines, schedule for September 18 and 19, at the Adelphia Hotel in Center City, Philadelphia. Jimmy Carter of Radio Station WDAS newsroom, a marine veteran serving as Public Relations Officer of the Reunion Organizing Committee, asked a question just before we arrived at the air terminal, "Brooks, when are you going to tell the real story of Montford Point Marines?" (We had been talking about Rhodes' novel, *The Chosen Few*.) My response was very terse, "Man, I've been too busy living the story of Black Marines!"

This was on September 18, 1965. Veterans had started arriving in the city from all over the country, for the two day reunion. We had run ads in black oriented newspapers, spot announcements on radio stations all over. And the response was most gratifying to the committee, for we had included the announcements in military publications, such as the *Navy Times*, *Leatherneck Magazine* and several marine base weekly papers. The response was tremendous from Chicago, New York, Washington, DC, from Boston, Norfolk and all the major Ohio cities.

On Saturday evening, the 19th, Sergeant Major Gilbert H. "Hashmark" Johnson and his wife, Eula, formally dressed for the dinner, came up to me during the reception. The Sergeant Major said, "Master Sergeant Gray, it was an act of Divine Providence that put you on recruiting duty in Philadelphia, to bring about the establishment of our fine Montford Point Marine Association!" Always the orator, Hashmark had a magnificent speaking voice; his statement to me was as if it had been made from the podium. Yet all of us who knew him recognized it as his natural speaking manner. In speeches, he would frequently make appropriate references to the Bible, to Shakespeare, to Churchill. In his address to the banquet dinner that evening, referring to the First National Reunion of Montford Point Marines, he concluded with the ringing declaration that, "it will be said that this was Hashmark's finest hour!" The audience of more than two hundred stood as one to cheer the Sergeant Major.

The unrestrained joy, the euphoria of being reunited twenty years after the kind of experience we had shared during World War II—this was evident in the faces of a few hundred men gathered at the Adelphia Hotel. This location, within two blocks of Philadelphia's City Hall, about seven blocks from Independence Hall and the Liberty Bell—only a few blocks further from the Tun Tavern site, where the Marine Corps had been founded 189 years earlier—this location would later lend credence to our banner "Born Here, Proud Here." Where the U.S.A. began. Black men from many parts of the country, reassembled, and proud of their service to America.

I wrote in "Remembrances From the First National Reunion" —more than twenty-seven years ago that, "On The Scene, Mrs. Henry Addison busily arranging the many banks of flowers all over the banquet hall . . ." She was assisted by other ladies, of course, setting the stage for this historic evening. From the very beginning, our wives, our ladies have been a most significant part of MPMA. That first evening, you could see it in their eyes, the same pride, the same joy their men were experiencing. I wrote

53

then that the flowers came from numerous visits to florists by Norm Triplett and Al Chappell. Actually, marine recruiter Staff Sergeant Triplett and Gunnery Sergeant Alex Chappell, of the 4th Marine Corps District, had visited eight or nine of the biggest funeral homes in the city—in Marine Corps staff cars and scrounged the "gorgeous flowers" after they had been used for dearly departed. Our budget for the reunion was so tight we would never have gotten off the ground, except for the government envelope mailings from my recruiting offices! Rooms at the Adelphia were $18.00, the banquet tickets, $7.00!

As I write this now in 1992, almost twenty-eight years later, I cannot emphasize enough the joy, the happiness on September 18 and 19, 1965, when Montford Point Marines were reunited again and feeling good! When many of us gathered on the morning of the 20th for breakfast, naturally the talk was about next year, August, 1966, for the first "convention" in Chicago. A lady from Xenia, Ohio said wistfully, "Oh, we'll have a great time next year —and great times in other cities in years to come, but it will never again be quite like this year."

The Reunion Committee was composed of a dozen Marine Corps veterans of World War II, several who were still on active duty, career Marines. Alexander Chappell of the Fourth Marine District made the most significant contribution to the effort, in putting together a national organization of the first black men to serve our nation as U.S. Marines. Henry H. Addison, a prominent West Philadelphia Realtor, made the next most meaningful service to establish MPMA. Addison had active duty in the Marines for three years during World War II. Obadiah Poe, a supervisory Civil Service officer at the Marine Corps Supply Activity (MCSA) on South Broad Street, was the very astute secretary of the organizing committee; Poe was elected secretary of the National MPMA on Saturday, September 19th. Addison was elected national treasurer, and served well in that position for seven years. James A. France, a Philadelphia detective who, like Poe, had been on active duty only during World War II, was the next most active member of the committee. France remained with a Marine Corps Reserve Unit, with active duty periods every summer; he retired after thirty years of such service. Jim France continues to be the most active member of MPMA (of the dozen who organized MPMA), currently the national Sergeant-at-Arms.

Norman A. Triplett, a native Philadelphian, who was also on Recruiting Duty in 1965, made important contributions to our effort that year. As chairman of the organizing committee, I was elected national president of the newly established Montford Point Marine Association. The five gentlemen named so far, were also elected national officers; France was First Regional Vice President. Attorney Arthur F. Earley, who immediately began to assemble the papers to file the Articles of Incorporation in the Commonwealth of Pennsylvania, was an active participant with the committee. And so, of course, was the legendary Montford Point Marine, Attorney Cecil B. Moore, in who's offices I made calls around the country, pulling the organization together. Cecil and Arthur were appointed Legal Counsel to the first administration. Leroy A. Dandridge, an extraordinarily knowledgeable Marine veteran of World War II, supervised the elections on September 19th; he was appointed national parliamentarian of MPMA. Most of us were officers and members of Penndelphia Detachment, Marine Corps League. Addison, Dandridge and France are Charter Members of this group, chartered in 1948— shortly after their release from World War II active duty, not long after their experience at Montford Point.

Alvin J. Banker, a well-known Montford Point Marine, a trained specialist in food administration, was another organizing committee member. In fact, Master Sergeant Al Banker was Mess

Sergeant at Marine Barracks, Philadelphia Naval Base in 1965. Staff Sergeant Leroy Mack of Electronics, Stock Management Division, Marine Corps Supply Activity, 1100 South Broad Street, Philadelphia, rounded out the MPMA organizing committee. I have named in this paper: Addison, Carter, Chappell, Dandridge, France, Earley, Moore, Poe, Triplett, in addition to Banker and Mack. Adding my name completes the dozen I have referred to earlier.

Of course, there are many other individuals in those early days who were central to making a success of the first National Reunion of Black Marines. It is important that I mention the names of some, but not all, of these original players: Willie W. Brown, the Sims brothers—Ervin and Carey, Joseph Wilson, Holsey Gillis, Sterling Gilliam, Fred Branch, Phil Herout, Cliff Hill, Clint Walters, Earl Smith, Israel Ray—all from the Philadelphia area. I must add Harrison D. Lockwood and John Hinkson.

And from Chicago: Albert Powers, Finis Henderson, Other Givens, Jimmy Hart, Sol Griffin, Warren Wright, Bert Potts, Harry Hamilton. I could easily name a dozen more from chicago; for these dear friends, some no longer living, were just terrific in sending names and addresses and telephone numbers of Black Marines in every part of the nation. the same for New York: Leonard, Fitchett, Tom Gourdine, John Hamlin, Art Gorham, Norman Sneed, Richard Holmes, curtis Johnson, Bill Hubbard, henry james, Harry Kanston, Beverly Starkey. From Norfolk: John Scott, Archibald Reyes; from Boston: jack Loving, Obie Hall, Chester Arnold, Frank Bispham; from Youngstown, Ohio: E. O. Britt; from Cleveland: Roy Buckner; from New Orleans: Gilbert smith.

I am frequently told, if you can't name everyone, don't name anyone. And, of course, I regard such advice nonsense. Those named here (and a few that I fail to recall) I consider the Founders of the Montford Point Marine Association.

In Richmond, VA, on March 10, 1944, I was sworn in as a United States marine. Departing by train the next day for Recruit Depot, Montford Point Camp, New River, NC, I sent my mother in Greenville, SC, a card from Richmond that read: "From the Halls of Montezuma to the shores of Tripoli, I'm on my way to Montford Point!" Less than two years earlier, the first black men *ever* had officially been permitted to join the U.S. Marines. I was well aware of what had developed over the course of more than ten years . . . going back to the 1930s when I delivered the *Pittsburgh Courier* (the national Negro-oriented newspaper) to homes in my native city, Greenville. Outstanding editors and columnists for *National Courier* included Prattis from Pittsburgh; George Schuyler from New York; a sociologist from Chicago, Horace Cayton; and the venerable historian, J. A. Rogers. The Pittsburgh Courier's Double Victory campaign in the early years of World War II was two-fold and simple: Victory over the Nazis and Japs and Victory over Jim Crow and bigotry and racism.

I had tried to enlist in the Marines as a 17-year-old in 1943, but was told I had to wait for my 18th birthday (in December), register for the Selective Service Draft; then, when called up, request assignment to the Marine Corps. Graduating from Sterling High School in Greenville in January, 1941—one month after my 15th birthday—I was working as a warehouseman at the Supply Depot, Naval Operating Base, Norfolk when inducted into the Marines. A friend who was to become my brother-in-law in July, 1944, Reginald Evans of Xenia, Ohio, had enlisted in the Marine Corps in 1942. Two professors from Sterling, D. J. Lenhardt and Giles Edwards, the coach and assistant coach of the football team, had enlisted early in the Marines, among the "chosen few." Another college man from Greenville, who I admired

57

very much, Frank Hall, was also in the Marines. All over the country, black men wanted to become a part of the elite Corps . . . our fathers and grandfathers and great grandfathers had been denied the opportunity—since the Corps was founded in 1775.

Boot camp at Montford Point was incredibly difficult. The Marine Corps has always exacted discipline by pushing the individual beyond limit, right from the start. In less than a week, I was writing my parents to "pray for me, that I might make it." When you hear a Marine vet say Boot Camp was a breeze, he speaks less than the truth—then, and in 1992. After three months of hell, the Montford Point graduate—like his counterpart at San Diego and Parris Island Recruit Depots, was so proud of himself, of his drill instructors; this experience remains with him for life, no matter whatever else he does. Upon completion of boot camp, I was assigned to the 52nd Defense Battalion; I knew that after recruit leave, I'd be on my way, with "my outfit" to the South Pacific!

While home on boot leave, one day I boarded a Greyhound Bus in Greenville to visit a girl friend in the mountain city of Asheville, NC, about sixty miles from Greenville. The bus was crowded, I was sharp in my tropical worsted Marine uniform, with the expert and sharpshooter badges affixed above the left pocket, and I was standing in the aisle, near the back of the bus. An attractive white lady motioned to the vacant seat beside her and said, "You can sit her, Marine." I thanked her and sat down, somewhat uncomfortable; for I had spent sixteen of my eighteen years in Greenville, SC, and knew well the back of a bus, the balcony for colored in the white theaters; I knew that segregation was the law of the land. The public drinking fountains, posted "White" and "Colored" a not uncommon sight in all of the South and in many cities in the North.

We had traveled not more than ten miles when I sat down, and I would see the white bus driver frequently look at me through the rear-view mirror. After another five or six miles, the driver pulled over on the shoulder, and leaving the motor running, came back where I was seated, and said, "You can't sit here. I'm sorry, but you'll have to get up." The lady protested, "I have no objection to this young man sitting beside me." He said, "I'm sorry lady. I don't make these laws, but I must enforce them." By this time, I was standing, seething with rage, thinking of what I could say that would dramatize the incongruity of me marching off to war in the South Pacific, yet being ejected from this seat. I said nothing. No one occupied the vacant seat, though several people remained standing. After another 25 or 30 miles, another white lady who had been near the front of the bus, came back and was seated. I was somewhat mollified, because I would have offered her the seat, if I was aware of her standing.

I want to present a similar story, two years later, when the war was over and I had returned from the Pacific. While awaiting discharge from the Marines, I had a weekend pass and visited Suffolk, VA, where I had been living when I enlisted. Returning to Camp Lejeune on a Carolina Trailways Bus, in uniform, I was seated beside a white soldier, also in uniform, and we had a delightful exchange, for more than an hour. He said to me that I should have been on duty in Italy, where he had been, that the Italian girls really liked the colored soldiers. I responded that women "like" any man who treats them with respect; that unfortunately, too many white G.I.s don't show girls at home or in foreign lands, the kindness or respect that women should be shown. Far too many white servicemen are crude and ill-mannered, I said. We were in agreement, on this point. Observations and comments I was to hear later, in Korea, in Japan, on Okinawa would affirm this early conclusion. Fellows telling me, or my overhearing foreign girls say, "I don't like white G.I.s; I prefer colored (or Black) Marines." And there was no objection from the white bus driver

59

of our being seated, Black and White, together, though segregation was still very much the law of the land.

The white soldier on the Trailways bus enjoyed telling stories
and I remember our laughter, when he told of Churchill visiting
Roosevelt at the White House, during the war. FDR saw
Churchill coming out of Mrs. Roosevelt's room one evening and,
from his wheel chair, roared, "Winston, I don't want any more of
that!" And Churchill, shifting his ever-present cigar to another
corner of his mouth, replied, "I don't blame you, Franklin; I don't
either!" Though barracks-humor and vulgar, obscene language is
commonplace with servicemen, and is perhaps understandable, I
hardly see the need for it to authenticate stories about the military. I have used this joke, for the soldier was aware that Black
Marines were known already as "Eleanor's Boys."

The Fair Employment Practices Commission (F.E.P.C.) and
Executive Order #8802 by Franklin D. Roosevelt in 1941, enabled
Negroes to be enlisted in the Marine Corps; enabled colored peo-
ple to be enlisted for general duty in the Navy. Mrs. Roosevelt was
in the forefront of the political war to bring about fair play, you
might even say decency, for minorities in the United States of
America. Black leaders such as A. Phillip Randolph, of the
Brotherhood of Sleeping Car Porters; Lester Granger, Executive
Director of the National Urban League; Walter White, NAACP
Executive Director; Marine Colonel Paul Douglas (who was later
to be Senator Douglas of Illinois), these and other "Liberal" leaders and organizations were influential in bringing about—and
establishing a climate for—Executive Order #8802, that started
the drive for equal opportunity for all American citizens. When
Lester Granger visited my battalion, the 52nd Defense Battalion,
and other military organizations throughout the South Pacific in
1945, we were on Guam. It was a large delegation of Navy
Department and Army officials, with leaders from industry and

civic organizations, who inspected the separate but equal facilities of men at war—to save democracy. The delegation would report and make recommendations to officials in Washington, DC of how the tensions could be eased. I remember among several of us Privates and Corporals and Sergeants, had concluded that Lester Granger was Father of Black marines, that Eleanor Roosevelt was Mother of Black Marines and this in a nation where miscegenation was still disdained.

Returning from recruit leave, the 52nd was scheduled to leave Camp Lejeune for Camp Pendleton, California in just a matter of weeks. I would have very little time to *snap in* as a Fire and Loader on the 40mm antiaircraft gun. I was assigned to "E" Battery, Light A.A.A. Group of the Defense Battalion. A couple of weeks bivouacked on Onslow Beach, along the North Carolina coast, firing the weapons every day at "sleeve" targets drawn by aircraft (or towed by boats), had our gun crews ready. Each Battery had four gun crews, consisting of the 40mm gun and Director; Elevation and Azimuth Trackers and Range Finder on the Director; the Gunner, Fire and Loader and ammo handlers on the gun itself. Each 40mm had a .50 calibre machine gun, with three men assigned to complement the crew. Men left behind when the 51st Defense Battalion had departed earlier formed the cadre that made the 52nd very professional. We were good. We were ready to vindicate ourselves as the best of the Marine Corps. The Navy Department and the marine Corps was pleased with our state of readiness. We were determined to show those guys of the 51st— who had set a few records firing at targets—that we were even better.

In addition to the Light A.A.A. Group, the 52nd Defense Battalion had a Seacoast Artillery Group, a Heavy A.A.A. Group (with 90mm Guns), Radar and Searchlight Batteries, a Headquarters and Service Battery . . . about 1500 men in the

61

Battalion, each group having communications and radar and other complementary equipment and school-trained personnel attached. I am also aware now, that I have not alluded to the before-dawn and long after sunset work, filling sandbags, building emplacements, for the guns and other equipment. In less than five months after my enlistment in the Marines, with the superb training regimen of the Corps, I was the professional marine Private, confident that with my associates and leaders, I was ready to meet the fore. I can never forget the last couple of weeks in boot camp, qualifying at the Rifle Range; nor the night firing at Onslow Beach; the tracer trajectories of gun fire, projectiles crossing in the darkened sky. Indeed, we were ready when we embarked by troop train for the seven day ride cross country for Camp Pendleton, CA. Just a brief stop there, then on to the Pacific Theatre of World War II Operations. Two years and a month after the first Black man had reported on board at Montford Point Camp, we were getting back reports from battles in the Pacific of the initial Black marine casualties, of bravery under fire. Our noncommissioned officers in the 52nd were all colored Marines, our officers, all white.

The following letters are the result of a request made by the author, for personal and/or known World War II experiences of former black Marines. One of the letters is that of a white Marine, Perry Fischer.

GUNNERY SERGEANT PERRY E. FISCHER
TURLOCK, CALIFORNIA

GUNNERY SERGEANT, MONTFORD POINT CAMP
8TH MARINE AMMUNITION COMPANY
U.S. MARINES 1940–1946

Note: This account is given from the prospective of one of the Special Enlisted Staff (SES) white NonCommissioned Officers of the, then, segregated U.S. Marine Corps.

This rather detailed account is the result of a combination of journal, diary and memory of Sgt. Fischer and it captures the real essence and portrays a vivid picture of the first black Marines during World War II.

The fact that Sgt. Fischer is white and has no ax whatever to grind, enhances the creditability of his story.

On April 30, 1944, I reported to the Commanding Officer, 8th Marine Ammunition Company at Montford Point. On the way to the company area, I noticed that almost all the Marines, those in uniform, were Black. Until then I had never seen a Black Marine nor did I know there were Blacks in the Marine Corps.

Several other white senior non-commissioned officers arrived at the same time I did at the company office. As we introduced ourselves to each other, they too revealed that they had not previously known of the Black Marines. Captain John R. Blackett, Commanding Officer of the 8th Marine Ammunition Company, assembled all of the white non-coms and officers who had arrived, and gave us a briefing on the activation of the company and the part we were to play in its development and future assignments.

He revealed that, up to that day, the Marine Corps had activated two Defense Battalions, twenty-six Marine Depot Companies (material handlers), and seven Marine Ammunition Companies. He also told us that two of the previously organized Marine Ammunition Companies, the 2d and the 4th, had seen combat, at Saipan. So did the 18th, 19th and 20th Marine Depot Companies. All reports had been positive as to their performance, and all of the lessons learned were to be applied during out training, because the 8th Marine Ammunition company was scheduled to participate in a large operation against the Japanese at a place to be disclosed later.

Captain Blackett then spoke to us about some "ground rules" that we, the white personnel, were to comply with when supervising the Blacks.

He emphasized that segregation was still the law of the land in the South, where we were, and that we had to insure that no incidents were to go outside of the compound but were to be reported to him immediately in order that he could resolve it within the company. He also told us that we were not to "fraternize" with the Blacks on or off post. To do so would make it difficult to maintain "Marine Corps" discipline. We were also told that there would be no "short cuts"—that Black Marines would be held to the highest traditions of the Marine Corps. These were proper and just rules, I thought, and went to sleep that night with the feeling that, even though I had experienced a sense of disappointment when I learned that I was to serve with Black Marines, I was uplifted by the fact that I had been specially chosen by a select group of officers for this unusual assignment. I resolved to do my best. I really had no idea of what was yet to come in this assignment, but I have lived to consider it the best assignment of my life, and came at a time when I could make a positive contribution to the Marines in fighting the war against Japan. More about that later.

The company was organized into three ammunition platoons and one headquarters and service platoon. Each platoon was led by a white second lieutenant, a white gunnery sergeant and a white platoon sergeant. A Black three stripe sergeant and a black corporal was also assigned to each squad. Our commanding officer was a captain. His executive officer was a white second lieutenant. Our first sergeant was white. In summary there were no Blacks who were placed above a white person in the company and that is the way it remained until the end of the war.

The first three days was a period of getting acquainted with each other; the Non-coms with their men, the Non-coms with their officers, the white non-coms with each other. There were twelve of us. We were all about the same age—24 to 28 years. None of us had been in combat. Our average time in the Marine Corps was six years. None were college graduates. All were high school graduates. In that respect, the Blacks had more that five college graduates in their ranks. About ten had some college. Ninety percent were high school graduates. Only one of the officers had seen combat, in Guadalcanal. We had a lot to learn, and for the most part, we had to teach each other.

Finally, there were the special enlisted staff (white non-coms). There was one characteristic we all had in common: none of us had seen combat. All of us had at least four years experience as a Marine. We were split even between the North and the South. Three were out and out bigots. The rest were not thrilled about their assignment, but, to be fair, their personal attitude did not affect their fairness to the men as Marines.

As for me, as a native of Chicago, where segregation was as rampant as it was anywhere in the South, but more subtle, I had made many friends of Blacks in Chicago and in Washington, D.C. during my four years of duty there.

It only took me a few hours to get over the "surprise" of being in a Black Marine unit. My problems came from my fellow white non-coms who couldn't tolerate the notion that we should treat the Blacks as equal, except for those instances where there flat out official rules and regulations that not only stressed segregation and discrimination, but severely punished violations of such official sanctions of prejudice and bigotry. But for survival, I had to enforce such rules. I hope I served as a buffer for many of my Black comrades in many cases. They deserved much better. I always felt the irony of the fact that Blacks tried for years to serve their country, actually had to fight to be allowed entry into the Marine Corps, fought their way through discrimination prevalent officially in the Marine Corps during World War II, died or were wounded in many cases on the battlefield, to protect the freedoms and democracy that was denied them. They were even denied the right to vote, yet the system gave them no relief from the artificial barriers established between them and their civil rights.

Well, through the foresight, perseverance, dedication, patriotism and pure hard work by such pioneers as Edgar Huff, "Hashmark" Johnson, for whom Montford Point was later renamed, Brooks Gray, Agrippa Smith, and others, a stream of well trained, well disciplined and motivated Blacks emerged from the swamps and parade fields of Montford Point to form the Defense Battalions, the depot storage units, and ammunition companies that subsequently served with honor and distinction in the Western Pacific. Now it was up to us, the special enlisted staff and officers of the 8th Ammo Company, to make our contribution to the war effort.

In May, 1944, the War in the Pacific was going full force. U.S. and Australian Forces had beaten the Japanese military back towards their homeland, but there were still some significant islands that had to be neutralized or taken before the biggest, and hopefully, the final battle could be launched, against the Japanese homeland. Black Marines were present in the South Pacific and Western Pacific, in Defense Battalions, and storage depots, performing like the expert Marines they were, but they were still waiting to get involved in combat. The remaining units at Montford Point were beginning to feel the heat of impatience to get out of the boondocks and onto the Pacific Island beaches. But even then, there was time for recreation, and the Black Marines took advantage of the opportunities as they became available, not frequently, but some was better than nothing.

After thirty days of running through the boondocks, and stacking ammunition boxes, the notion of getting back to civilization, even for just a few hours, was incentive enough to assure perfect conduct, excellent test scores, and super inspections. The company was divided into two sections, A and B. One-half of each platoon was designated Section A, and the other half was designated as Section B. On alternating weekends, one section went on an overnight liberty, while the remaining section remained at the camp to perform what duties had to be performed, such as guard duty, mess duty, latrine duty, and cleaning of equipment and weapons. Even though a Marine was eligible for liberty, he might not always take advantage of it. Lack of funds was probably the main reason. Being married and not wanting to fall victim to temptation may have been another reason. The harassment the Black Marines faced in town, even while in a Marine Uniform, was another compelling reason for many of them to pass up liberty.

The nearest town to Camp was Jacksonville. It was only a small city then, dependent on the business the Marines from Camp Lejeune brought to it. But until 1942, only white Marines were seen in the town's bars, restaurants and theaters. When the Black Marines went into Jacksonville for the first few times, they were met with the full force of segregation and racial discrimination. As a result, the Black Marines sought to go beyond Jacksonville to larger cities, where there were more facilities for Blacks.

Meanwhile in Jacksonville, the Blacks who had no choice but to spend their free hours there, were reminded constantly that Blacks, whether Marines or plain citizens, had to follow the rules of segregation. The policy of the military camp was to provide Military Police, one white Senior Non-commissioned officer and one Black Sergeant. We went into Jacksonville in a jeep whenever we had Black Marines on liberty. After checking in with the Jacksonville Police Station, we would patrol the streets, drop into bars where Blacks frequented, checked to see that the Black Marines wore their uniforms properly, were not drunk or disorderly, or got involved with the white population to the detriment of the military camp. We also had jurisdiction over the white Marines, but in case a white Marine was involved, the Black MP who was with the White MP was instructed to stand back and let the White MP resolve the problem. I saw this with my own eyes and much to my shame, was a party to this unconscionable support of racial discrimination by the officials of the town council and the military establishment. At one time, the civilian bus drivers who drove the buses from Jacksonville to other cities near enough for the Black Marines to visit on liberty, would not allow the Black Marines on their buses until all the White Marines had boarded. Many times Black Marines had to wait until the last scheduled bus left Jacksonville, and often some of them were unable to eat on that bus. When our Commanding Officer learned of their predicament, he ordered military buses into Jacksonville for the exclusive use of the Black Marines. The buses stayed with these men until they were to return to camp. Eventually, this despicable situation was remedied, but only because of near riots.

The situation on the camp was not much better. There was a separate, and believe me, not equal club for the Black enlisted personnel. There were no Black Officers in the Marine Corps then, so there was no Black Officers' Clubs. Their club was poorly furnished, located in an old wooden building, poorly ventilated in the summer and poorly heated in the winter. The club was closely supervised by members of the White Special Enlisted Staff. Closing time was strictly enforced. Drinks per person were closely controlled. Women were permitted only on special occasions. I can certify that, at that time, a Black Marine was treated like a second class citizen. I have heard some whites protest that White Marines in Recruit training were treated the same way, but this is not quite true. In spite of the constant deprivation, harassment and oppression, almost without exception, the Black Marine maintained his dignity throughout training and eventually did rightfully claim the admiration of their fellow White Marine leaders, especially those who served with them in a combat situation. If I had been subjected to the types of indignities they were subjected to, I seriously doubt that I would have been able to cope with the situation and perform as well as they did.

To a casual observer of the 250 Black Marines who were seen standing at attention in uniform, he might say, "they all look alike" and they do, from a distance! But, as we white Special Enlisted Staff were to learn from the very beginning of our training with the 8th Ammunition Company, each of the Black Marines were unique individuals. Each had their own peculiar life experience, education, desires, goals, attributes, needs, capabilities and special reasons for wanting to be a Marine; they were different from any other individual, like fingerprints. As our training

69

progressed together, the Special Enlisted Staff came to recognize these unique characteristics, and used them as strengths to build the company. Prejudice may have been present, but we were no fools; we recognized skills and talents beyond measure. Why waste them? After all, our life might depend on them soon. These men were from all walks of life: students, business men, ministers, salesmen, truck drivers, clerks, farmers, teachers, coal miners and more. Most were single. About thirty percent were married and had children. Their ages ranged from seventeen years (or less) to at least thirty-eight years. All had passed recruit training with a commendable degree of efficiency. It was obvious that their Black Drill Instructors had done their job well too. Their efforts and accomplishments sure made our job easier.

For one thing, the Black Marines, without exception, were in great physical shape. Fortunately, I, too was, because in the mountains where my last duty was, I had to run up and down the trails everyday before breakfast: participate in long marches with full pack, and take part in all kinds of sports. And speaking of sport, the Black Marines of our company were among the best at the camp at that time. We won a lot of inter-company games in baseball, track, volleyball and touch football. I had a modest degree of talent in baseball and volleyball, and barely qualified for the teams. Other off-duty diversions included a choral group that could make tears come to one's eyes as they sang the popular songs and spirituals of those days. We also had several talented musicians who played horns, guitars, flutes, clarinets and all kinds of pseudo drums such as table tops, tin cans, backs of chairs, and one real set of drums. Saturday nights the area to the rear of the company was the scene of many a "hot night in the old town tonight" music festivals.

Through these on and off duty activities, the 8th Ammo Company build up a camaraderie that was to last throughout the fifteen months we were together. By the time we completed our advanced training at Montford Point, we were a close-meshed, effective fighting machine, a company of lean, mean, hungry Marines! I am sure that we owed a great part of our success to the "Buddy System." I think we were very good as a total ammunition company. All we lacked was practical application in a real situation. We had self confidence, but were not cocky. We had eliminated much of the racial problems within the company. The White enlisted and officer staff had been accepted by the Black Marines of the company and the special enlisted and officer staff had great admiration and respect for every man in the company based on their response to the training. We weren't perfect, and probably not the best company to graduate from Montford Point, but you better not have told us that to our faces at that time.

Finally, Graduation Day did arrive, in late August 1944. All men were granted a seven day leave before departing for overseas. Only a few were unable to go on leave, for personal reasons. We had a graduation parade where we were allowed to "show off" our marching skills and brand new dress greens. All but twenty-four of the privates were promoted to PFC, several were advanced to Corporal and Sergeant. We didn't know exactly where our company was going, but scuttlebutt had it that our first stop was Hawaii, for six months advanced training in combat operations of an ammunition dump. And were we ready? You bet!

While the Eighth Ammo Company was completing its advanced combat training at Montford Point, Black Marines were already under enemy fire in the Western Pacific. The Third Marine Ammo Company was among the first Black units to take part in combat operations in World War II. Also, the 18th, 19th and 20th Marine Depot Companies were right there with them. Their target was three islands of the Mariannas Group that were vital to the U.S. Military advance towards Tokyo. These were

Saipan, Tinian and Guam. D–Day was June 15, 1944. Almost all of the Black Marines landed on the beaches of Saipan on that day.

The first Black Marine casualty of this campaign was PFC Leroy Seals of Brooklyn, N.Y. who was with the Third Ammo Company. He was wounded only a few hours after his landing. He died the following day.

There was also a lot of activity against the enemy during the night of June 15. According to the company commander of the 18th Marine Depot Company, a platoon attached to the 3rd Battalion, 23rd Marine Regiment landed on Blue Beach One, right on the heels of the first assault waves. As the 18th Marine Depot Company Marines spread out on the beach, an enemy mortar shell exploded within twenty-five yards of the platoon. Four of the Black Marines were seriously wounded and evacuated. Captain William N. Barr, commanding officer of the 18th Marine Depot Company, reports,

> Mortar shells were still raining down as my men unloaded ammunition, demolition material, and other supplies from amphibious trucks. They set up 'security' to keep out snipers as they helped load casualties aboard boats to go to hospital ships. Rifle fire was thick as they rode guard on trucks carrying high octane gasoline from the beach. A squad leader killed a Jap sniper that had crawled into a fox hole next to his. They stood waist deep in surf unloading boats as vital supplies of food and water were brought in. . . . There were still a few scattered snipers still on the beach. My men accounted for several of these.

When the 20th Marine Depot Company went into the battle, the commanding officer's orderly, Private Kenneth J. Tibbs, of Columbus, Ohio, was killed. He was the first Black Marine fatality of World War II as the result of enemy action.

In addition to the casualties in the Ammunition and Depot companies, two Black Marines of the First Stewards Branch, working in areas normally considered "safe" and "behind the lines," received leg wounds.

As a result of their brave actions in the Mariannas, the Commandant of the Marine Corps was quoted as saying, "The Negroes are no longer on trial. They are Marines, period."

All four of the Black Marine Companies that served at Saipan and Tinian were included in the Presidential Unit Citation awarded to the Fourth Marine Division. The Navy Unit Commendation Ribbon was awarded to units of the Second and Fourth Marine Ammunition Companies that participated in the Guam Campaign while attached to the Fourth Marine Division as support.

By September 15, 1944, the Marine Corps campaigns in the Western Pacific Theatre of Operations were no longer a purely "lily white Marines only" war. Blacks and whites, side by side, on the beaches and in the fox holes, worked, fought, slept, bled and died together, dependent on each other. A new, proud and indelible tradition was born. Blacks forever would have a history of bravery, devotion to duty and outstanding achievement to set standards for Marines of all colors.

About the same time, with Black Marines already on the firing line, the 8th Marine Ammo Co. was en route to a date with their destiny. Even then, another fierce and deadly Marine Corps campaign was taking place in which Montford Point Marines were again storming the beaches defended by Japanese soldiers. This time it was the island of Pelilieu in the Palau Group. Another battle flag for Montford Point.

The 11th Marine Depot Company and the 7th Marine Ammunition Company, in support of the Fourth Division stormed the beaches of Pelilieu on 15 September 1944. As the Japanese guns, rifles and mortars swept the beaches, the Black Marines, still aboard ships off shore, served in the ships' platoons unloading the vital battle supplies for the run to beaches. Soon after, they were called to the beaches to move those same supplies and ammunition to the Marines fighting on the front lines. They also helped evacuate the wounded while still under fire.

The first Black Marine to be wounded at Pelilieu was Private Dyrel A. Shuler of the 7th Marine Ammo Co. Two days later, eight more Black Marines were wounded by enemy fire. The 11th Marine Depot Company went on to suffer the highest casualty rate of any Black Marine unit in World War II.

The excellent performance and bravery of the men of the 11th Marine Depot Co did not go unnoticed. The 7th Marine Ammo Co. also drew attention for their efforts in the same campaign. Major General William H. Rupertus, commanding the first Marine Division, sent identical letters to the Commanding Officers of both companies, which stated:

> The performance of duty of the officers and men of your command has, throughout the landing on Pelilieu and the assault phase, been such as to warrant the highest praise. Unit Commanders have repeatedly brought to my attention the whole hearted cooperation and untiring efforts exhibited by each individual.
>
> The Negro race can well be proud of the work performed by the 7th Marine Ammunition Co. [11th Marine Depot Co.] as they have demonstrated in every respect that they appreciate the privilege of wearing a Marine uniform and serving with Marines in combat. Please convey to your command these sentiments and inform them that in the eyes of the entire Division that they have deserved and earned a 'well done!'

What magnificent accomplishments by the relatively new Corps of Black Marines! The misery, racial discrimination, and undue harassment, suffered while trying to become a real Marine, which, even while under he "best" conditions is a challenge of the greatest degree, did not deter the Black Marines from serving their country as they always knew they could. But they weren't through yet! There was one more great challenge ahead for Black Marines, some say the greatest of all the Marine Battles in World War II, and I and the Black Marines in the 8th Marine Ammo Co. were going to not only have a front seat in the campaign, but were going to make our presence well known on the battle stage. The 8th Ammo Co. hadn't caught up with the fighting war yet, but it was on the way!

Leaving Montford Point, knowing that our next destination was somewhere in Hawaii, provoked no tears at the departing. The situation for the Black Marines could only improve. Since Hawaii was not a state of the United States, there would be no "Colored" or "Whites Only" signs there. Excitement was high, anticipation great!

The trip by train westward across the United States took three full days, almost nonstop. We all tried to relax as much as was possible aboard a troop train that was crowded with men and equipment, but the ingenuity of the Marines was boundless. Without help from outside (the train was a "sealed train," that is, there would be no stops for track side vendors), everything we would get would be aboard the trains before we left Montford Point. Only the porters would be allowed to depart the train at water stops long enough to get newspapers and magazines, but for no other reason. During the trip, the marines were still responsible to keep their rifles clean and their field equipment in good order, and that helped to pass the time. Most of their leisure activity consisted of card games, shooting dice, cribbage games and reading.

There was always music: singing, instrumental music and the ever present harmonica. The NCOs were assigned compartments that were converted to sleeping rooms in the evening. The rest of the troops were assigned to troop train accommodations that could be made up into hanging bunks similar to those aboard a troop transport ship.

The most looked-forward-to activity of the day was meal time. Although there was little exercise aboard the train other than "punishment push-ups" for minor infractions, appetites seemed to increase well over normal. We ate mess hall style. The food was cooked in large pots just like in the mess hall and dished out, cafeteria style, on trays which were then carried back to the seats. It was a good arrangement because it fed a lot of men quickly. Food was hot, tasty, plentiful and varied enough to fill everyone's taste. On the second day out, however, a glitch appeared in the train's refrigeration unit and all the perishable foods, especially the meat, became inedible. It was all thrown away. The officer in charge of the "mess hall" informed us that the train would take on provisions in St. Louis, Missouri, about seven hours away, but that sandwiches, coffee and fresh food would be available for lunch. I was amazed at how many candy bars, cookies and cokes appeared from the men's back packs and sea bags to supplement their makeshift lunch. Spirits remained high, and we looked forward to the rest of the trip. As promised, fresh food was loaded aboard the train at St. Louis, and, in order to make up for the inconvenience, we were served steak, chicken and hot pastries at all of the remaining main meals. We even had bacon and eggs for breakfast the next day.

At the end of the third full day, close to midnight, the troop train carrying the 8th Marine Ammunition Co. arrived somewhere near the train station in Oakland, CA. Meeting us were about twenty army 2 1/2 ton trucks converted to carry troops.

Each of the trucks was driven by a female truck driver. We loaded aboard and were soon on our way to Treasure Island for further transport to Hawaii by ship. Those of us who rode in the front seat of the truck (rank has its privileges) were fascinated by the sight of the bridges, which even in the relative blackout, could be seen in all their famous glory in the moonlight. I have never forgotten that view.

About forty minutes after departing the train, we arrived at dockside at Treasure Island Naval Yard. There, waiting to take us aboard, was a quite large Kaiser Liberty ship, converted to carrying troops. It promised the Marines hot showers, hot meals, proper sleep, movies and time to write letters home. We were not the only Marines aboard the ship. Two other depot companies, a pioneer platoon, some units for replacements for a Marine Aviation Unit, and various other type skilled marines were also aboard. The ship was overloaded, it turned out, but every bunk was filled.

Perhaps the most welcomed "luxury" we enjoyed was the opportunity to go to the ship's Exchange. One man from each platoon cold take a list and go every day we were at sea. Main items we sought were candy bars, shaving gear, souvenirs and pens. We couldn't buy beer or coca colas.

The first thing that all of the 8th Marine Ammunition Company did when they got aboard the ship was to locate our bunks and then take a hot shower, the first since leaving Montford Point. After the shower, we were permitted to go to the messing area for a hot meal since we hadn't eaten since early that afternoon. By 0200 hours, we were all back in our bunks and fast asleep.

Reveille aboard ship was 0730 hours, and even though we arrived late the evening before, we too were gotten up. All the units aboard ship were assigned meal schedules which allowed every unit to eventually be first in line for chow, a very fair system.

77

Unfortunately, in as much as we were the last unit to board the ship, we were the last to eat that morning. But in the long run, we didn't mind. It was one of the best breakfasts we all had since joining the Marine Corps.

Life aboard a troop ship follows a strict routine: "Going topside" while the areas below deck were cleaned then going below deck while the "topside" was cleaned. Twice a day! Even on Sundays! Sleeping all day was impossible even though it was not prohibited. I said it was a guise to keep us from getting bored.

We always had physical training after we cleaned our bunk areas and ate breakfast. It consisted mostly of running in place and pushups. Our weapons were inspected every other day. Otherwise we pretty much had the run of the ship except where prohibited. We later learned, the ship carried a lot of equipment such as jeeps, weapons, tents, food and other war items for the troops in the Western Pacific.

As I indicated earlier, the food that was served to us was excellent. It was plentiful, properly cooked and there was a wide variety of meats and vegetables. Coffee, tea and milk were available all day long. So were snacks like donuts, cookies and small cakes. We all had to take turns in the mess, but that was more a privilege than a duty. The Naval personnel, especially the cooks, were quite nice and amiable towards the men.

One of the chores the Special Enlisted Staff had to perform aboard ship was to conduct a class for their respective platoon in aircraft identification. We were subject to both submarine attack and air attack from the Japanese, and we had to be able to know the difference between friendly and enemy attacking forces. It also helped to fill in the hours. We never however, had to use that knowledge en route to Hawaii.

What did the men do most of the time when they weren't involved with required activities? Again, game boards, cribbage, craps, poker, even bridge, reading, writing letters and just gazing out across the beautiful Pacific Ocean. A couple of the more enterprising men rigged up some fishing gear in an attempt to catch anything from a shark to a whale. There were some success- es (small fry) and those who were lucky were able to get the ship's cooks to cook the fish for a few of the friends of the lucky fisherman.

Once a day a ship's newspaper was circulated which brought us up on the course of the wars in both the Pacific Theater and the European Theatre of Operations. Marines, including Black Marines, were engaged in fierce warfare in the Marianas, but the number of Marines killed and wounded were never revealed to us.

Time passes fast when one is having fun. Therefore, almost before we were aware of where we were, some one spotted Diamond Head off our bow and we all cheered—now we were in the Hawaiian Islands at last! Another step in the direction of the battlefields. We passed the Honolulu Towere, a landmark for years for passengers of the famous Matson Lines, and in about an hour anchored at Ford Island in Pearl Harbor. We passes the site of the Japanese attack on the Navy Fleet on December 7, 1941, and could still see all of the iron hulks of the sunken battleships. It was a grim reminder of the audacity and ferocity of the Japanese, and the sight was quite sobering to say the least. We debarked our ship, loaded again on truck transports, and shortly after were liter- ally dropped off at out Hawaiian home for the next six months. It was called "Camp Catlin" and exists today by the same name.

Arrival at Camp Catlin culminated in what we later referred to as our Pacific Ocean excursion from San Francisco to Honolulu. Life aboard ship was heaven compared to life with the 8th Marine Ammo Company at Montford Point. Even though everyone enjoyed the seven day vacation aboard ship, we were glad to set our feet back on solid ground, especially when that solid ground was to be the shifting sands of Waikiki Bach.

Another advantage the assignment to Camp Catlin would bring us was the end of cramped quarters, endless lines waiting for food and Post Exchange privileges and having to take our turn for the latrines. The hard sidewalks of Honolulu, the shining lights of shops and theaters downtown, and the smell of ginger leis was ever in our minds as we rode on the back of the 2 1/2 ton trucks, again driven by women, to our new albeit temporary home at Camp Catlin.

It took about fifteen minutes to make the trip from Pearl Harbor to Camp Catlin. As we passed through the front entrance of the camp, we could see that the facility was quit large. There were rows of wooden barracks for many blocks. Most of the Marines we noticed in the barracks area were also Black Marines. Our hopes that segregation was to remain in the United States was dashed. Racial discrimination was an integral part of the Armed Forces and was to remain so for many many years more. Eventually, we arrived at a section of the camp that was reserved for the 8th Ammo Co. and we debarked. Each platoon was assigned to one barracks. Each barracks was two stories, and accommodated half of one platoon on each of the floors. Single bunks lined the walls, as a pleasant surprise, all of the bunks were neatly made up with sheets, blankets, pillows and pillow cases. Wall lockers and foot lockers were situated adjacent to each bunk. At one end of the floor was a small section that included a book-case filled with magazines, books and newspapers. We called this our day room area. There were also some small tables with chairs where we could write letters or study.

At the other end of the floor were the washing and toilet facilities, the showers and a small utility closet. Adjacent to this area was a small room that was to serve as a squad room for the two Black Platoon Sergeants. The accommodations were simple but comfortable.

The company headquarters was located next to the three bar-racks. Behind the company headquarters was the company supply facilities. I think we had four jeeps, sundry office equipment and furniture, armorer's equipment for maintenance of weapons and other Table of Organization equipment. While at Camp Catlin, our weapons were stored in this building under lock and key for security reasons. They were issued to the men on Saturdays, prior to inspection, for cleaning and maintenance and then returned after inspection.

The officers were billeted at the Officers' Quarters located in the Marines Transient Center, another large marine military facil-ity adjacent to but separated by barbed wire from Camp Catlin. The Transient Center was a camp for "Whites Only." Hawaii was a territory of the United States at that time. It had not attained statehood yet and was a racially free territory. However, all of the military facilities in the Islands were still segregated by military law, hence the separate facilities for the Black Marines. Ten years were to pass before the integration of the military forces were ordered and effectively enforced.

A consolidated mess hall fed all of the marines in the camp, including the Special Enlisted Staff. Approximately eight hun-dred men were served at each meal. The food was adequate, plen-tiful and somewhat varied. This was important because the work we were to do was "hard labor"; we had to move ammunition and ammunition boxes weighing often close to or more than one hun-dred pounds each. We could, if we wished, supplement the meals served with a visit to a small post exchange where candy bars were available at a very low price, and many of us did.

Finally, as at Montford Point, there was a black enlisted men's club. It was definitely not equal to the white enlisted men's club at the Transient Center, but I recall how the Black Marines worked hard on their own initiative to create an atmosphere which was good for them and which gave them a place to get out of the barracks on the nights they could not leave the camp. A theater was also available, and we did see some first run moves from time to time.

Perhaps the best morale builder for the Black Marines was the privilege of leaving camp for liberty in Honolulu and its suburbs. City buses ran right past the camp so transportation was no problem. Liberty was restricted to the weekends and holidays; half of each platoon alternated with the other half so that there was always half of the company available at the camp. The Black Marines were well received by the civilian population of Hawaii. Because the Black Marines were well behaved, friendly, very respectful of the women and generally well liked by the Hawaiian men, they provoked very little trouble. If there was any problem, it usually took place between the white sailors and marines. I don't recall there being any major incidents, but anywhere there is inter-service rivalry, regardless of color, there will be altercations. Hawaii was no exception. But it was great to see the artificial barriers of segregation disappear whenever a Black Marine exited the camp.

Liberty and recreation was a secondary goal of the 8th Marine Ammunition Company. It was sent to Hawaii to prepare material and ammunition for combat, and to prepare itself for combat against the Japanese. There was plenty of opportunity to do both during the six months we were at Camp Catlin. Each platoon was assigned to work at separate locations in and near Pearl Harbor where ammunition had been stored. Our job was to inspect it, renovate it if appropriate, package it, code it, stack it on pallets so it could be easily loaded and unloaded, and transport it to ammunition ships in the harbor. Only a few of us and the officers knew at that time, the destination of the ammunition, code name Operation Detachment, but it wouldn't be very long before all of the men knew.

Several days a week, the workday was shortened to allow the platoons to participate in company formations, inspections, classroom training, lectures and orientation on field sanitation, personal hygiene and security. We also received immunization shots for cholera, smallpox and other diseases. We were issued completely new field equipment, additional sets of camouflaged battle fatigues and new weapons.

By the end of the first month at Camp Catlin, a new positive spirit seemed to engage the entire company. It seemed to be more cohesive, more confident than it ever had been. We knew what we were doing! The hard work we were doing made our muscles harder and stronger. The white officers took a real interest in the progress of all the Marines and were present in our day to day activities much more than ever before. Positive personalities heretofore unknown to each other began to emerge between the Black Marines and the Special Enlisted Staff; as a result the units were having fun doing work. I believe that because we no longer were fresh recruits but well trained Marines now, we were anxious to prove our mettle, and everyone, I mean, everyone in the company gave their best effort.

There was a break in the normal routine on September 7, 1944. All marines at Camp Catlin participated in an Awards and Decorations ceremony, either as members of the marching units or as spectators. Depot Companies 12, 17, 21, 22 and 24 and the Sixth Ammunition Company were the marching companies. Because of its recent arrival, the 8th Marine Ammunition Company and several other recently arrived depot companies were present as spectators. The honorees were Black Marines of units that had participated earlier in action against the enemy in Western and Central Pacific Theater of Operations. This included Depot Companies, Ammo Companies and members of the Stewards Branch. The awards for bravery, meritorious action against the enemy, and Purple Hearts visibly impressed all of those present at the review. It was cause to reflect, if we, the newest of the units comprised mostly of Black Marines, would do as well when our turn came. These brave Marines certainly set the standards for others to follow, and became an indelible part of Black Military History.

Slowly but surely, time passed. We anticipated our sailing orders daily, and remained in a state of readiness at all times. During October, November and December, we experienced several "alerts" but they proved to be exercises only. Nevertheless, our Commanding Officer spoke highly of the response to alerts by the unit. Christmas 1944 arrived and passed. Scuttlebutt (rumors) kept us all in a state of agitation. We were headed for either Formosa, China, the Philippines, Okinawa or even Japan. But events in early January, 1945, made us look at each rumor carefully.

Our work shifts were cut in half. We worked mornings only. In the afternoon we concentrated on maintaining our equipment and weapons, assured our officers that every marine had his full allocation of all required items. Our officers spent almost all the time together with the platoons. They intensified the lectures on enemy aircraft, ships and personnel identification, Field Security, Sanitation and self-defense. We even learned that the code names we had stencilled on the pallets and boxes of ammunition and shells was for the operation we were headed for, but Operation Detachment's actual identification was still a secret to all but the officers and a few senior NCOs.

Finally, on or about January 10, 1945, our loading orders came. Carrying full field equipment, including helmets and gas masks, we moved to Ford Island, where we had disembarked when we first arrived in Hawaii. This time we loaded aboard Landing Ship Troop (LST) Number 970. Only the first and third platoons boarded this ship. The second platoon boarded LST Number 641.

There were marines, sailors and members of the Navy Construction Battalion units on the ship also, and sever platoons of Depot Companies. The LST was loaded with all kinds of equipment and ammunition, small arms, and large artillery and mortar shells. All men were aboard by 1800 hours when we ate our first meal. Again, we ate cafeteria style, but there was nothing fancy about what we ate, or where we ate the food. We used our field equipment and canteens all during the trip. There were no bunks. An LST has no sleeping facilities for the troops it carries. We used our field blankets and slept wherever we could find space. The eternal lines for the latrines and showers appeared again. We could only shower every three days with salt water with a ten second rinse with fresh water, sometimes. Drinking water was rationed. The trip from Hawaii to Operation Detachment was not going to be a vacation cruise. This trip was going to be a real test to see how cohesive the 8th Ammo Co. really was. But thanks to such men as Sergeants Tom McPhatter and Lawrence Berkley, Corporals Ralph Blara, Gil Brooks, Thomas Hall, Otis Henry Sr. and PFC Ellis Cunningham and many others too numerous to mention, we had organization and discipline throughout the trip. Although every inch of space was utilized for supplies, the men found room to play the inevitable games of craps, poker, cribbage, bridge, rummy, checkers and some games I never found names for. Many of us caught up on writing letters which were picked up from time to time by boats from other ships in the convoy, which in turn delivered mail to us.

Our LST was only one of approximately 800 ships comprising the Fifth Amphibious Corps. Aircraft carriers, battleships, cruisers, destroyer, mine layers, oil tenders and many other auxiliary vessels sailed with us from the Hawaiian Islands. Since an LST is the slowest of all ships in the navy, we were always at the rear of the convoy. Even though we carried explosives on the LST, we never saw any other ships during the entire forty day trip to Operation Detachment until we were about twenty miles from our destination, which we did not know until a few days before 19 February 1945. It was still Operation Detachment for us.

The Special Enlisted Staff and the officers spent their time inspecting weapons and equipment, continuing identification of enemy aircraft and personnel, and leading the units in physical training. The biggest burden of keeping the troops occupied and busy in essential tasks was left up to the Black sergeants and corporals and they did a magnificent job in maintaining discipline and morale. They all got on well with the navy men on the ship and for the short time we were on the ship, the color of the person's skin was no longer significant. I can't speak for all of the other white personnel, but I am sure the great majority of them were, as I was, proud to be associated with these new marines.

We did learn about our destination on 15 February 1945. Operation Detachment was Iwo Jima, a little pork-chop shaped island about six hundred miles south of Japan. It had been the target for many months for aircraft bombing and naval shelling, but the damage inflicted on the island was unknown. Someone had estimated there were about 20,000 Japanese soldiers and marines defending the island. The island was only about five square miles in area. There were beaches on both the eastern and western sides of the island, but we were probably going to land on the western side because the surf was too high on the eastern side. We finally got to see a mock-up of the island and saw that at the southern end was a volcano (extinct) about 550 feet high that overlooked the rest of the island. The northern part of the island was mainly a plateau with scarred, twisting gorges and broken by ridges 340 to 368 feet in height. Between the northern plateau and the volcano, named Mount Suribachi, was a plain covered with black volcanic ash. The whole island, we learned, contained hundreds of pill boxes, caves and other concealed gun positions, including the sides of the volcano. Three airfields, two completed and one under construction, was the main objective for the 70,000 Marines, sailors and other personnel. The 8th Marine Ammunition Company was to supply ammunition to three marine divisions, the 3rd, 4th and 5th. The 33rd, 34th and 36th Marine Depot Companies were to provide the labor for the movement of hundreds of thousands of tons of material and supplies from the ships to the beaches, and if necessary, to the three divisions on the firing lines.

In all reports of the Battle for Iwo Jima, the most prominent story told is the raising of the American Flag on top of Mount Suribachi on D plus 4. That was the 23rd of February, 1945, four days after the initial landing on 19 February 1945. We all were witnesses. The two platoons of the Eighth Marine Ammo Co. aboard LST 970 were kept busy at sea off shore of the beaches readying the ammunition on board for movement to the beaches. Several times before D plus 4 the LST beached to dispose of needed ammunition to shore parties as called for. The Second Platoon, led by 2nd Lt. Frances J. DeLapp, disembarked from LST 641 on D plus 22 and assisted the shore parties moving supplies. On that day, Lt. DeLapp and Corporal Gilman D. Brooks were wounded and evacuated. Three days later, PFC Sylvester J. Cobb, also of the Second Platoon, and Corporal Hubert E. Daverney and Private James M. Wilkens of the 35th Depot died of wounds received on the fire swept beaches.

Three other Black Marines from the 34th Depot Company were hit on 25 February 1945: Sergeant William L. Bowman, PFC Raymond Glenn, and Private James Hawthorne, Sr. A Black Marine replacement, PFC William T. Bowen, was also wounded then. The 34th Company's last casualty in February, PFC Henry L. Terry, was wounded the next day.

Every Marine who set foot on the island from D–Day, 19 February 1945, until 11 April 1945, the day the 8th Marine Ammunition Company left the island, was always vulnerable to enemy fire. There were more Black Marine deaths and casualties to come.

All of the platoons of the Eighth Marine Ammo Company landed by D plus 4. Our mission—to establish the Marine Ammunition dump for the three Marine Division—became operational on D plus 4. We wasted no time settling in. Each platoon was divided into two twelve hour shifts. While one half of each platoon went right to work setting up the bunkers in the area designated for our dump, the other half started digging fox holes in the volcanic sand outside the dump. This was a most difficult task since digging a hole in volcanic ash is like pouring water into a sieve. For every shovel of ash dug, two more seem to slide into the hole made by the first shovelful. However, there were some ingenious men in the platoon, and in just a few minutes various techniques were applied like using the wooden pallet from the ammunition shipments made the foxholes secure. Attached to our company were several Construction Battalion engineers who operated bulldozers. The bulldozers were used to dig bunkers in which the ammunition and shells could be safely stored. If ammunition in one bunker was to be blown up, the ammunition in nearby bunkers would most likely be protected from simultaneous detonation. At least, that was the theory. It soon was tested.

Our ammunition dump was located approximately five hundred yards north of the base of Mt. Surabachi, and about the same distance south of the first Japanese airfield, known as Motoyama No. 1. Although the American Flag had been raised the day before, there were still Japanese snipes in caves on the sides of the volcano. Some marines worked in the bunkers; others moved in and out with trucks and other vehicles, loading and unloading the ammunition. During all this activity they would be peppered with sniper fire. This continued for several days after the volcano was considered "secured." Meanwhile, the dump and the foxhole area were also subject to artillery and mortar fire of the Japanese who were still in possession of the central and northern section of the island. We were frequently exposed to such fire for the next two weeks.

Except for 1st Lt. Kenneth Graham, who had seen combat at Guadalcanal in 1942 as a Gunnery Sergeant, every Marine of the Eighth Ammo Co. receive his baptism of fire in the first few days of the assault.

Even as we were debarking from the LST, 20mm shells from Japanese guns on the island began to fall around us. I remember that we barely noticed them because they seemed to "pop" rather than make a large explosive noise. Soon, someone yelled, "take cover," but no one in our platoons was really concerned at the time. Later when we had time to think what had happened, the reality of war fell heavily upon us, and from then on, we never had to be told "take cover" when the shells began to fall.

No marine of the 8th Ammo Co. had it easy for the next twenty-five days. Every moment was filled with work, or sleeping. Under normal conditions, ammunition handling is a laborious task. Working with little or no equipment, having to battle the sliding volcanic ash that got into everything and hindered our work, and keeping our eyes and ears open for sniper fire and possible artillery shelling, our hands became bloody, scraped and sore.

Early in the morning of March 2nd, 1945, the war came to the 8th Ammo Co. full blast. At about 0200 hours, a Japanese artillery shell hit our ammunition dump, which by this time, was crammed full of explosives. We had at least twenty bunkers full. The shell hit a large mass of white phosphorous shells and 81mm mortar shells filled with high explosives, touching off a chain reaction that sent explosives hundreds of feet skyward. A giant mushroom cloud of acrid smoke blanketed the southern third of the island, where we were laced by crazy trajectories of multicolored signal flares, rockets, phosphorous shells and grenades. Artillery and mortar rounds detonated in a rolling thunderclap that roared on and on. Machine gun and rifle bullets crackled like thousands of giant fire crackers exploding in an endless string. One of the men from my platoon ran over to where I was as we were trying to fight some of the fires near one of the bunkers. "Gunny, it's like I always thought Hell would be like!" he cried.

It only took a few seconds for all of the men of the 8th Ammo Co. to get out of their foxholes and over to the Ammo bunkers to see what was going on. At first, most of us thought we were being over run by banzai Japanese, but we didn't see any of the enemy. Flares above showed that some of the fires were very close to the entrance and exit of the dump, and some of us thought we might be caught in a fire trap or hit by exploding shells. Some of the Black Marines, without being ordered to do so, jumped onto some of the idle bulldozers, and along with some Seabees, began to attempt to extinguish the fires or cover the unexploded ammunition with volcanic ash, ignoring the danger to themselves. Other Black Marines grabbed hold of some of the hot canisters and bundles of ammo and separated them from those which had not been hit. For about forty minutes, there were bunkers that were burning so furious and shells exploding so frequently, that we had to vacate the bunker area. It was indeed an inferno like Hell at times. In spite of a false alert that a poison gas attack was imminent (some one had misinterpreted a white phosphorous artillery shell that had exploded), and the approach of a lone twin-engine Japanese aircraft about 0245 hours which just kept on flying by, Marines of the 8th Ammo Co., Marines of the nearby Depot Companies, and Seabees billeted nearby worked continuously for the next four hours, attempting to prevent additional fires and explosions and salvaging the remaining ammunition so that supply to the marine divisions in the northern and western parts of the island, still in the midst of ferocious fighting, would have the ammunition it needed. Ammunition from the dumps on the beaches never stopped arriving at our dump. It took about a week for things to get near normal. We worked at least eighteen hours a day, and some of the Black Marines even more, to get back to being a fully operating ammo supply dump. The training we had participated in at Montford Point and in Honolulu paid off. Many of the men had burns on the hands and face, flesh seared by the heat of the fire. PFC Melvin Thomas, one of the hardest working and highly motivated men in my platoon, was killed during the explosions. Private William L. Jackson was wounded and evacuated. On 8 March, Private J.B. Saunders was wounded by shell fire while on the beach.

The 8th Ammo Co. had now won its battle colors, but paid a dear price for it. This however, was not the last occasion that the mettle and training of the Black Marines of the 8th Marine Ammo Co .and the Depot Companies was to be tested.

Early on 26 March, ten days after Iwo Jima was officially declared secure, a well-armed column of 200 to 300 Japanese, including many officers and senior NCOs slipped past the marine infantrymen who had them holed near the northernmost airfield and launched a full scale attack on the army an marine troops camped near the western beaches. These U.S. troops were unarmed, waiting to be transported off of Iwo Jima. However, in the same area, units of the 8th Field Depot, including some from the 8th Ammo Co., Depot Companies and 5th Pioneer Company responded immediately, using their weapons and hand grenades. The attack began approximately 0300 hours in the morning of the 26th. It was had to tell friend from foe in the dark and the action was wild and furious. I was working in the dump area and could hear and see some of the firing. Later, I learned that the 8th Ammo Black Marines as well as those from the Depot Companies were in the thick of the fighting and took part in the mop-up of the enemy remnants at daylight.

Again, the 8th Ammunition Company suffered casualties. PFC Harold Smith died of wounds received in the fight. Corporals Richard M. Bowen and Warren J. McDaugherty were wounded but survived. Private Vardell Donaldson of the 36th Depot Company was wounded and subsequently died as a result of his injuries. PFC Charles Davis and Private Miles Worth, also of the 36th Depot Company were wounded but recovered later. Two members of the 36th Depot Company, Privates James M. Whitlock and James Davis both received Bronze Star Medals for "heroic achievement in connection with operations against the enemy."

The commander of the Corps Shore Part and 8th Field Depot Company, Colonel Leland S. Swindler expressed his pleasure with the actions of the Black Marines in this battle, and in his report for Iwo Jima stated that he was:

> highly gratified with the performance of these colored troops, whose normal function is that of labor troops, while in direct contact with the enemy for the first time. Proper security prevented their being taken unaware, and they conducted themselves with marked coolness and courage. Careful investigation shows that the displayed modesty in reporting their own part of the action.

Later in the day of the action, I had a chance to talk to the two white special enlisted staff senior non-commissioned officers of the 1st Platoon of the 8th Ammo Co., Platoon Sergeant Lowell E. Smith and Gunnery Sergeant Desmond H. Johnson. They spoke in glowing terms of the men of their platoon and their brave conduct while repelling the Japanese suicide group. I am certain that many of the Black Marines performed in a heroic manner and under normal circumstances, would have been recommended for medals for bravery; unfortunately, they weren't.

Publicity of the action of the Black Marines on Iwo Jima, both in response to the ammunition dump explosion and the repelling of the Japanese suicide attack received very little publicity in American Newspapers and Magazines. I have researched every possible document I could get my hands on, and found only a few brief mentions. But I can tell the world, being there at the time, that the Black Marines at Iwo Jima indeed represented their people proudly and bravely, and made their mark in history, not only in the Marine Corps, but for all Black Servicemen in all branches of service in World War II.

These men, who worked, fought, were wounded and died under the American Flag, who had been treated as second class citizens all their lives, who had to fight segregation to get into the Marine Corps so that they could fight the enemies of America— they did this while still stereotyped as second class citizens. But they showed that they were First Class Americans in the jungles of the Solomon Islands, on the beaches of Saipan, Tinian, Guam, Pelilieu, on the sands of Iwo Jima and on the heights of Okinawa. I recently had a communication from Lt. Col. Lemuel W. Houston, USMC, who served at Iwo Jima as corps beach master under Colonel L. S. Swindler.

> The Black Marines of the ammunition and depot companies at Iwo Jima had a tough, demanding and dangerous job but like all Marines, they did it well. Despite treacherous tides and hostile shell fire which seriously handicapped the ship-to-shore operations. The depot companies kept supplies

moving inland for the support of our troops. There
was never a shortage of ammunition due to the
valiant efforts of the ammo company. And when
the Japanese launched a 1st-ditch attack on these
men, they proved once again that they were true
Marines by repulsing the attack.
Hard training and high dedication paid off when it counted.

Most of the Black Marine units at Iwo Jima departed the
island on or after April 11, 1945, the day before President
Franklin D. Roosevelt died. The Eighth Marine Ammunition
Company returned to Hio, Hawaii to recuperate, reorganize, take
on replacements and prepare for the next big assault. I remained
with the company until August, 1945.

When the war ended the Eighth Ammo Company was aboard
another transport ship, combat alerted for the planned assault on
Japan. I returned to Pearl Harbor because my enlistment termina-
tion was coming up. The rest of the company went on to perform
occupation duties in Sasebo, Japan and Tientsin, China. It was
deactivated on September 17, 1947 at Guam.

After Iwo Jima, the next and last major assault in which Black
Marines from Montford Point took part in was the Battle for
Okinawa.

The largest number of Black Marines to serve in combat took
part in the seizure of Okinawa, on the Ryukyu Islands, the last
Japanese bastion to fall before the atomic bomb and the threat of
invasion of the homeland combined to bring the war to an end.
Three ammunition companies, the 1st, 3rd and 12th; four depot
companies, the 5th, 18th, 37th and 38th; of the 7th Field Depot
arrived at Okinawa on D–Day, 1 April 1945. Later in the month,
the 20th marine Depot Company came in from Saipan; in May
the 9th and 10th Depot Companies arrived from Guadalcanal, the
19th from Saipan.

Many of the Black Units were used in some landing exercises off the southeast coast of Okinawa to deceive the Japanese. Assault troops of the Tenth Army (III Amphibious Corps; and the Army's XXIV Corps) actually were landing on the western coast of Okinawa at the narrow waist of the sixty mile long island. By this feint, the Japanese commander might be fooled into keeping his troops on the eastern coast away from the actual landings on the western coast.

On 3 April, most of the black troops landed on the island in support of the 1st and 6th Marine Divisions which comprised the III Corps. They met little opposition on the beaches or in the first few days after their landing.

Many of the casualties suffered by the Black Marines occurred in April, when their camps and work areas were still relatively near the front lines. The Fifth Marine Depot Company lost three men because of wounds: PFC Willie Hampton on the 6th, Private Therrance J. Mercier on the 15th, and Private Eldridge O. Oliver on the 28th. The 1st Ammunition Company had two men wounded, PFC Thomas Early on the 10th and PFC Joshua Nickens on the 15th. The 38th Depot Company had one man wounded, PFC Alvin A. Fitzpatrick, on 27 April. One of the Black Marines assigned to the Officer's Mess of the 29th Marines, Steward's Assistant 1st Class Joe N. Nryant, was wounded on 5 April, and in the 1st Marine Division's Headquarters, Steward's Assistant 2nd Class Ralph Woodkins caught a shell fragment in his face on April 12.

The Battle for Okinawa further tested the mettle of the Black Marines of the depot and ammunition companies as the Tenth Army started to drive south against the well dug-in Japanese defenders. It was difficult for the support units to keep up with the advancing army, especially as the spring rains turned the already too long transportation routes into quagmires. The Black Marines served multiple functions, moving supplies forward and carrying wounded and casualties to the rear. Casualties among these Black Marines lessened but still continued. Private Arthur Bowman, Jr. of the 12th Ammunition Company the last of the Montford Point Ammunition Companies, and Private Charles L. Burton of the 3rd Ammunition Company were wounded in May; PFC Charles H. Jackson of the 3rd Ammunition Company and PFC Richard E. Hines of the 10th Depot Company were wounded in June.

The Black Stewards in Corps, wind, division and regimental headquarters, many who volunteered as stretcher bearers when the fighting was heaviest, did not go unscathed. Steward 2nd Class Warren N. McGrew, Jr. was killed and shell fragments wounded Steward's Assistant 3rd Class Willie Crenshaw of the 1st Division on 9 May. Four days later, two men in the 6th Division, Cook 3rd Class Horace D. Holder and Steward's Assistant 3rd Class were both wounded in the same manner. On 26 May, three stewards of the 29th Marines Headquarters, Steward's Assistant 1st Class Joe N. Bryant, Steward's Assistant 3rd Class Jerome Caffey, and Private Morris E. Clark were all wounded. Bryant's second wound in the campaign gave him an unsought after "first" among Black Marines. Two thousand Montford Point Marines served on Okinawa. They left their mark and a lot of their blood there. They added materially to the tradition of bravery and honor of not only the Black Marines who had preceded them in World War II, but to all of the Marines in the 215 years of Marine Corps History!

I recommended strongly that any one interested in a fuller and exciting report of the extensive contribution of the Black marines in Okinawa obtain a copy of "Blacks in the Marine Corps," a publication printed by the Historical and Museums Division of the Headquarters, Marine Corps.

In 1965, a group of the first Black men accepted into the Marine Corps met in Philadelphia, Pennsylvania at the Adelphua

Hotel at 13th and Chestnut Streets. They formed an organization called the Montford Point Marines Association, Inc., and elected Master Sergeant Brooks Gray, U.S. Marine Corps Recruiter at that time, as its first president. Other elected officials were Henry Addison, a prominent West Philadelphia realtor, National Treasurer; James Frances, a detective, was named Regional Vice President; Leroy Dandridge was named National Parliamentarian; Attorney Cecil B. Moore and Arthur Earley were appointed legal Advisors.

Many chapters since have been formed throughout the United States, and National Conventions have been held in major cities where chapters exist, such as Chicago; New York; Cincinnati; Atlanta; Washington, D.C.; Los Angeles; Cleveland; San Francisco and Detroit. The 1992 National Convention, which will be the 27th Annual Convention, will be held July 12–19 at The Town and Country Hotel, located in Mission Valley, in San Diego.

Sergeant Major Gilbert "Hashmark" Johnson, for whom Montford Point was renamed Camp Johnson in his honor, had a great love and high regard for the Montford Point Marines Association. He often referred to this organization in glowing terms.

Following is an extract from one of his most dynamic speeches and is the best expression of the purpose and goals of the organization:

> The Montford Point Marine Association, Inc. was issued a National Charter by the Court of Common Pleas, Commonwealth of Pennsylvania in 1966. The purpose of this organization and its subordinate chapters are as follows:
>
> To promote and preserve the strong bonds of friendship born from shared experiences in the

U.S. Marine Corps, especially those of the original Negro marines, who served during the period 1942–1951 and onward to the present day.

To devote ourselves to the furtherance of those friendships as Marines, both active duty, honorably discharged and retired, through the sharing of experiences and accomplishments and to ensure harmonious relationships whenever possible.

To provide encouragements for the utilization of the leadership qualities among our youth, consistent with democratic principles of our society.

To promote efforts toward self improvements as individuals and to further the interests the country and the association.

To promote higher education through scholarship grants.

To promote due recognition, meaning and loyalty to the Constitution of the United States and of the State of North Carolina, or any State in which we reside . . .

Under the guidance of its founders, Brooks Gray, its first national president, and still active as president emeritus, Montford Point Marines Association, Inc. has developed into one of the most respected and effective military service organizations in the United States. It is now open to members of all military services as associate members. Recently, Lamar Golden, one of the honored members of the association was named National Commandant of the Marine Corps League for 1992.

The Montford Point Marines Associate, Inc. is committed to helping honorably discharged or retired veterans of all branches of the service in their transition from military to civilian life. The Association is recognized by the Department of Defense as a non-profit organization and as an advisory and investigative facility for bad conduct discharges awarded to personnel upon their separation from the military service.

Sergeant Major Edgar Huff, whose brilliant Marine Corps career has few rivals, is still a positive influence on the conduct of Marine Corps Association Business.

All Black Marines join an honored tradition, marked by blood, sweat and tears of marines, Black like themselves, who had to fight to break the barriers against Blacks, fought segregation within the Marine Corps while trying to become the honored marines they did become, when they joined the Montford Point Marines Association, Inc.

I firmly believe that the struggle for recognition for Black Marines, and for Black Servicemen of all military branches of the Department of Defense, would be "forgotten" or intimidated at the least, if the Montford Point Marines Association, Inc., had not been created when it was, and not managed by those pioneers of Montford Point over the past twenty-seven years.

As a white, former U.S. Marine who served at Montford Point from May to August 1944, and subsequently with the Black Marines of the 8th marine Ammunition Company in Honolulu, Hawaii and from 19 February to 11 April at Iwo Jima, and finally in Hilo, Hawaii from May to August 29, 1945, I am indescribably proud and honored to have had the distinct privilege to be a part of the tradition of Black Marines in the Marine Corps. If I could know that only one Black Marine felt that I made a positive contribution to their well being and dedication to the Marine Corps, I feel that all my efforts were worthwhile.

This I know, without questions, if I had been trained in boot camp and in advanced training under the same segregated conditions and severe conditioning that the veterans of Montford Point had been trained, I doubt if I could have met the challenge to the extent that they did, but I believe they are all better Marines for sticking with it. I am glad that some of them were on my side at Iwo Jima, where we were together, side by side, together through hell.

Finally, I would like to quote from a letter I received from Brigadier General T. V. Draude, Director of Public Affairs, U.S. Marine Corps, dated July 11, 1991.

"The Marine Corps will always remember the unflagging courage, devotion to duty, and unfailing willingness to serve as displayed by those Marines that trained at Montford Point during the outset of World War II."

CORPORAL CURLEY MCCLELLAND
BRADDOCK, PENNSYLVANIA

7TH MARINE AMMO COMPANY
SECOND CASUAL CO. HOBN.
MONTFORD POINT, CAMP LEJEUNE
1944–1946

I enlisted in the Corps on my 18th birthday, but didn't have to report to the camp until January 4, 1944. That is a day I will never forget. I am from the state of Pennsylvania, and really didn't know too much about being Jim Crowed against, although we had it here, but not as the southern states. We left home—that is four white buddies and I, we all went to school together—we were allowed to travel together until we got to Washington D.C. There we boarded a train headed for North Carolina. We were separated to different cars, white car and nigger cars, then as the train approached Rocky Mountain Depot, the black porter came thru pulling down shades and told us to get down on the floor while the train was stopped there; we soon found out why because a couple pop bottles and bricks came sailing thru the windows. White sailors threw them. We were allowed to get back in our seats once we were out of the station. Then we got to Wilson about 6 o'clock in the morning. There was no one there to meet me; you can imagine how alone I felt. So I went into the bus station trying to get some information about Camp Lejeune, Montford Point.

I was then told that I couldn't get a bus until later on that morning. When the bus did come I was told to get on board and that it would take me to Montford Point, but instead it took me to Hadnock Point, the Women's Base, and at that time it was all white. There I was, a lonely black boy in the middle of a white women's camp, and deep into the south. I showed my orders to a white officer Marinett; she put me on a bus that took me to Jacksonville and let me off.

I had to walk about three miles to Montford Point. I didn't mind, just to see some black faces was good enough for me. But at first they treated me almost as bad as the whites, but I guess they were doing their job. We were put in a receiving area for about a week. I was told to make the heater red hot in the shower room, which almost caused it to catch fire—causing me to get in a lot of trouble, that was in January. I finally got put into a platoon #328 Co. F.; we were under a Sgt. Wright, our company leader. My drill leader was Corporal Carl Hamilton, who would treat us like men. Our other battalion leader was Sgt. Maj. Wright, who we nicknamed "the spider." We were also under a Sgt. Maj. E. R. Huff, who went to make a name for himself along with Hashmark Johnson.

After our boot camp training of about nine weeks we were given a short leave of eight days, and two days of that was traveling time.

When we arrived back to the camp we were put in a regular Co. with the 7th Marine AMMO Co. Then we underwent a short training period, May thru June, that taught us the different sizes of ammo and bombs, and a little about demolition.

July 1st, we Boarded ship at New Port News, and headed out for the South Pacific. We went thru Panama Canal on to New Herdidies, and from there to Guadal-Canal, so for the rest of July and August we trained some more and then joined up with the 16th Field Depot F.M.F., then with the 1st Marine Division, and went on to the Peleliu invasion, which was in September thru October 1944, until the island was secured. We lost a few good men. I don't understand why we never really got any recognition on our part as being Marines; I am still looking for the answers.

We went to Saipan, Guam, for a spell and then returned back to the USA in May 1946, at which time I was discharged on May 9, 1946.

All of our officers were white, as well as our NCOS. The highest rank we could achieve was Sgt. Major. Sgt. Maj. Huff treated us like men; we would meet up in Jackson in the evening, have dinner and a couple of beers, which made our day.

Thru it all it was tough back then, but I wouldn't trade it for nothing; it really made men out of kids. Like the saying goes: Once a Marine, Always a Marine.

I could tell you a lot more . . . I am still actively trying to get us some recognition. I will close out for now, God Bless You.

Yours Truly,
Curley McClelland
Semper Fi

Once a Marine, Always a Marine

LETTERS

508 Talbot Avenue
Braddock PA 15104
September 30, 1991

Hi Fred,

Just a few lines to let you hear from me. I'm fine and hope this letter finds you likewise. I was glad and surprised to hear from you so soon.

I get a little excited when writing or talking about times in the Corp.

I hope I gave you a little something to go on. I asked you about Perry Fischer; he is white and a major in the army. He retired and went into the Marine Corps as a private, then worked his way back to Sergeant. He was in the 8th AMMO Co.; they went on the invasion of Iwo Jima (he can tell you some stories.) He was also working for recognition of the Black Marines of WWII, 1942–1945.

I am sending you a couple of letters. After you read them, my other old friend, Corley, really has an interesting story to tell. I am also passing your address on to some old timers who were in the

Corps 42–45. I hope they can pass something on to you. Do you remember when our DI would come for bed check late at night and would catch someone smoking, and he would make us get our sea bags and fall out and run about ten laps? It would be cold, but we had it to do.

When we went to the movies the little balcony was so small couldn't but about two people get up there—one time was enough for me. I remember they were putting on a USO show—so you know they had white women of course—some of the guys started cat calling and whistling. The white boys got mad, but when the name nigger came out—we almost had one of the worst race riots. Somehow the word got to the Island Command, and broke it up real fast. He made it clear to everybody that those shows were for everybody, and if you didn't like it, stay away because he was not taking no stuff, from black or white.

They always warned us bout going to town and getting hold of that hot stuff. I guess you heard of the name of Boone Dock Shorty; she was real, would burn you and we would get punished for it "brig time." I guess our best time was when Lt. Troupe wrote that song "Take Me Away From Jacksonville." Everyone sang that song.

Well I will close for now. Here is hoping to hear from you soon, and may God bless and take care of you.

Once a Marine, Always a Marine

Semper Fi

Sincerely,

Curley McClelland

Both of the following letters were published by Leatherneck *Magazine as Letters of the Month:*

LETTER TO THE EDITOR
SOUND OFF DEPARTMENT
BLACK HISTORY MONTH

Dear Sir:

February commemorates the 46th anniversary of the Iwo Jima invasion. It is also Black History Month. I was a gunnery sergeant with the 3rd Platoon of the 8th Marine Ammo company that participated in the assault on Iwo Jima in 1945.

Like the 33rd, 34th and 36th Field Depot Companies, we were all part of the 8th Field Service Depot trained at Montford Point, New River, N.C.; and except for a small, special enlisted and officer staff who were white, the remainder of us were black Marines.

I am now and have been frustrated and concerned to learn how little is known and acknowledged by both high-ranking military personnel, present and past, and by the public in general, of the major contribution these black marines made to many of the victories in the Pacific during WWII. When you consider that they were not even allowed into the Marine Corps before June 1942, and only a few were permitted as mess stewards prior to that date, their efforts in such a short time before commitment to combat situations to learn the "Marine" way, and to distinguish themselves later in the islands, is nothing short of heroic. Yet, there are only a few literary records to this effect, and it is commendatory that *Leatherneck* has helped to correct this shortcoming.

However, recently, I located and read another book written by a former marine and Korean vet whose brother was also a marine who made the supreme sacrifice. Chuck Lawliss, who was a combat

107

correspondent, has written a fantastic book, *A Marine Book: A Portrait of America's Elite*.

The book is thorough, accurate, comprehensive and true to the Marine Corps spirit. It covers the story of Marines from beginning to present. But more to the point, it gives appropriate acknowledgement and credit to the Black Marines of the Corps.

In contrast, I read *Coral and Brass* by General Holland M. Smith, of his experiences in the Pacific during WWII as leader of the Marines in many battles (Peleliu, Saipan, Guam and Iwo Jima) where black Marines participated. Incredible as it seems, General Smith did not make a single mention of Black Marines.

To me, this is unconscionable, yet reflects the attitude of a major portion of Americans even to this date. I don't mean to diminish his leadership abilities, but only to point out his insensitivity to about 18,500 Black Marines, many of whom were wounded, killed and earned medals for bravery and heroism.

That is why I appreciate *Leatherneck*, Chuck Lawliss and the few others who have not forgotten the most "invisible" Black Marines.

Perry Fischer
1830 Loyola Way
Turlock, CA 95380

Perry Fischer served as a Marine gunnery sergeant from 1940 to 1946, and retired from the U.S. Army as a major in 1962. S.O.Ed.

Letter to the Editor
Sound Off Department

Dear Sir,

I want to thank *Leatherneck* and also Sergeant Major Edgar Huff for the story "Paving the Way" in the February issue, and for telling it like it was, being a Montford Point Marine.

We had to fight for the right to fight. My experience being among the first Black Marines seemed to be synonymous to the Civil War movie *Glory*, as very little had changed as far as prejudice when I entered the Marine Corps during WWII.

I am sorry that the name "Montford Point" was changed to Camp Johnson, even though Sgt. Maj. Hashmark Johnson was a Marine Corps legend, especially among Montford Point Marines. These first black Marines who fought, worked, sweated and died throughout the Pacific campaigns have lost some of their Marine Corps roots by the name change.

I feel the Marine Corps could have given Sgt. Maj. Johnson another award or form of recognition. As a World War II Marine, I will always think of myself as a Montford Point Marine, not a Camp Johnson Marine.

I did not know either Huff or Johnson, as both were already overseas when I was in boot camp, and when I went overseas, they were back stateside.

After I reenlisted at the end of World War II, I was sent to communications school and graduated as a telephone lineman and message center specialist (2511). Our outfit went to Saipan, Marshall Islands, to relieve elements of the 52nd Defense Battalion and take over their equipment. Our designation was Heavy Antiaircraft Artillery, Provisional, and the only combat unit left on Saipan.

Our area was between Tanapag and Marpi Point air base, across from the Japanese POW compound. We were guarding

2,000 prisoners while they were waiting to be repatriated back to Japan.

Soon after we sent the Japanese home, we were told to fall out, and a white lieutenant colonel told us our outfit was to be disbanded. We were to become a depot outfit and sent to Guam. We boarded an LST and went to Guam. When I arrived, I was by my lonesome and was integrated into a white outfit (H&S, 5th Service Command) as a telephone lineman.

I guess there was a shortage of linemen, as this was before the services were integrated. However, I was billeted in the all black 49th Depot area and given a recon to drive to work every morning. My white co-workers were okay. I felt I needed a buddy, and I was joined by another Black Marine named Venters, from Texas. We'd gone through communications school together. We worked as linemen until I was discharged.

The pride of being a Marine overshadowed all the prejudices of the time. Somehow, I survived. Maybe Montford Point boot camp did that?

Averine Corley
2819 Ralston Ave.
Indianapolis, IN 46218

Profiles of a Living Legacy
1945 and Beyond

FREDERICK C. BRANCH—formerly an enlisted man of the 51st Defense Battalion, was commissioned a second lieutenant as a reserve officer, the first black man to do so. While Branch immediately went on inactive duty, he stayed active in the reserve. He commanded a black volunteer unit in Philadelphia in 1949 and returned to active duty during the Korean War. Dr. Raymond B. Floyd was one of several other enlisted marines who did not qualify for the Officer Training received by Branch.[38]

Dr. Floyd has something to say about this matter in his story found elsewhere in this book.

> This did not sit well with black Marines in general because shortly before, three other seemingly well educated college graduated marines failed to make the grade at Quanticos 9th Platoon Commander Class.[39] These three included Charles F. Anderson, Sergeant Major of Montford Point Camp; Charles W. Simmons, former Sergeant Major of the 51st Defense Battalion and First Sergeant George F. Ellis, Jr. They became later in civilian life a lawyer, a college professor and an

author and physician. What's more, three more similarly qualified black candidates that followed failed to make the grade at officers training.[40]

In 1946, HERBERT L. BREWER of San Antonio, Texas was commissioned a reserve officer on inactive duty along with two other Black Marines. He served on active duty in the Korean War and in 1973 was a reserve colonel in the Philadelphia area, the highest ranking black officer in the Marine Corps Reserve.

In 1948, WILLIAM K. JENKINS from Elizabeth, New Jersey, a contract NROTC graduate from Illinois Polytechnic Institute and a navy veteran of World War II was commissioned a reserve second lieutenant and assigned to inactive duty. Lieutenant Colonel Jenkins, in 1973, a reserve Lieutenant Colonel was called to active duty in the Korean War where he became the first black officer to lead marines in combat as both a weapons and a rifle platoon commander with Company B, 1st Battalion, 7th Marines.

In 1949 the first black woman Marine, ANNIE E. GRAHAM, enlisted at Detroit, Michigan. The following day, ANN E. LAMB joined at New York City. The third black woman to join was ANNIE L. GRIMES of Chicago who later became a chief warrant officer.

Researching stories of black Marines in the Korean War became increasingly difficult because of the end of segregation. Records pertaining to Black Marines aside from strength and deployment statistics, became virtually nonexistent. As a consequence, information on Black Marines during the 1950s and beyond has been extracted from the experiences and reminiscences of officers and men with whom I talked whose careers span these years. There simply were no unit records because there were no black units.

In 1952, SECOND LIEUTENANT FRANK E. PETERSEN became the first black Marine pilot, receiving both his wings and his commission at Pensecola, Florida. Flying the attack version Corsair, Petersen completed sixty-four combat missions in Korea earning the Distinguished Flying Cross and six air medals. In 1973 he was the senior black regular officer in the Marine Corps as a Lieutenant Colonel.[41]

Most black officers commissioned during the war were reserves who were released to inactive duty after completing a normal tour, but a few like Petersen stayed on to become regulars.

In 1953, RENNETH H. BERTHOUD, JR., of New York City was the second officer to receive a regular commission. He was a graduate of Long Island University with a major in biology. He was designated a second lieutenant in the reserve in 1952 and a regular officer in 1953. He served as a tank officer in both Japan and Korea. In 1973 he was a lieutenant colonel assigned to Headquarters Marine Corps in the Installation and Logistics Department.[42]

HURDLE L. MAXWELL enlisted in the Marine Corps during the Korean War after three years at Indiana State Teachers College and was commissioned a reserve second lieutenant also in 1953, and six months later was made a regular officer after completing the Basic School at Quantico. He too served in both Korea and Japan as a tank officer. As a lieutenant colonel in 1969, he became the first black officer to command an infantry battalion, 1st Battalion, 6th Marines. Lieutenant Colonel Maxwell retired in 1971 after serving on active duty for over twenty years.[43]

It was impossible for these men to be inconspicuous wherever they served; in fact they were marked men so to speak. They represented Black Marines as a group and whatever they did, and how they performed, their job was to many indicative of what could be expected from Black Marines in leadership positions. While all black officers in the 1950s were mostly junior in rank, there were a number of blacks in the top enlisted pay grade.

EDGAR R. HUFF was one such black. He established a string of unbeatable firsts for Black Marines. In September 1952, he became the gunnery sergeant and then the first sergeant of Weapons Company, 2nd Battalion, 8th Marines at Camp Lejeune. On February 1954, he became the battalion sergeant major, the first black to hold such a position in an infantry battalion. At the end of 1955, Huff became the barracks sergeant major at the Marine Barracks, Port Lyautey, Morocco. An interesting sidelight to his promotion is that the white master sergeant, who had been sergeant major of Port Lyautey and who had not been selected for the higher rank, said he would rather retire than serve under a black man. Headquarters Marine Corps retired him as soon as he could be returned to the USA.[44] Huff continued in later assignments through the 1950s and 1960s to become regimental sergeant major at Camp Lejeune and Okinawa. These advancements were not always smooth as he recalled later regarding his service in the 2nd Force Service Regiment: "I did everything I could to get along with these people and maintain the dignity of the position and it was very difficult to do this."[45]

JAMES F. JOHNSON, an outstanding and talented man, did much to change the image of the Steward's Branch. Many young blacks felt there was a stigma attached to being an officer's steward, a dead end specialty that was limited to blacks.

Johnson emphasized the positive side of the duty at the same time teaching advanced techniques of cooking and serving and management pointing out the salability of the craft in civilian life. He also encouraged them to get involved in off duty educational courses. Johnson retired as chief warrant officer in 1965. Shortly afterward, he received his Bachelor of Arts degree; later to be joined by a Master of Arts degree; he then went on to work for both juris doctor and PhD degrees. In civilian life he became a successful insurance salesman. A California State Commissioner of Veteran's Affairs, a Vice Chairman of the Federal Civil Service Commission, and the Assistant Secretary of the Navy for Manpower and Reserve Affairs. All this was accomplished in the space of eight years by a man who had entered the Marine Corps in 1944 as a private with a record book stamped "Colored" and an enlistment contract "Steward Duty Only."

THE VIETNAM WAR

While the Black Marine was well represented in the Vietnam War, it is very difficult to estimate the number of decorations he earned: Navy Crosses; Silver Stars, Distinguished Flying Crosses, Bronze Stars and many other medals were won by these men for heroic action and Meritorious Service. But in one category of awards (The Medal of Honor), however, there is no doubt about who and how many were recipients. Five Black Marines were awarded the Medal of Honor during the Vietnam fighting. Each man for "Conspicuous Gallantry and Intrepidity at the risk of his own life above and beyond the call of duty." All used their own bodies in the thick of a fight to shield the blast and fragments of enemy grenades from their comrades; all perished in the selfless attempts. For the first, PFC JAMES ANDERSON, JR., it happened at Cam Lo on February 28, 1967.

He was a rifleman with Company F, 2nd Battalion, 3rd Marines. His home was Compton, California. On September 6 of that same year, SERGEANT RODNEY M. DAVIS of Macon, Georgia, a platoon guide in Company B, 1st Battalion, 5th marines sacrificed his life during heavy fighting in Quang Nam Province. PFC RALPH H. JOHNSON of Charleston, South Carolina on 5 March 1968, while serving as a scout with Company A, 1st Reconnaissance Battalion, saved the life of one of his comrades at the cost of his own.

On February 23, 1969, PFC OSCAR P. AUSTIN of Phoenix, Arizona, an assistant machine gunner with Company E, 2nd

Battalion, 7th Marines was killed while protecting a wounded man from enemy grenades and rifle fire. The fifth Black Marine to be awarded the Medal of Honor was PFC ROBERT H. JENKINS, JR., of Interlachen, Florida, while serving as a machine gunner with Company C., 3rd Reconnaissance Battalion on 5 March 1969 defending Fire Support Base Argonne south of the demilitarized zone.[46]

Throughout the years of the Vietnam war Black Marines did their duty in combat, but many took issue with the Corps as they found it outside of battle. Victims of discrimination in civilian life, the young blacks were justifiably suspicious of the military system in which they found themselves. They were quick to find or infer discriminatory practices.

Leaders of the Marine Corps became increasingly concerned about the sometimes abrasive projection of the discontent of these young blacks. Effective measures to eradicate this problem would have to be taken. And they were. This effort would be toward nothing short of complete elimination of discrimination, even "the appearance, however unintentional, of discrimination."[47]

This was a far cry from the situation facing the first Black Marines who reported to Montford Point Camp in August, 1942. Joining a segregated Marine Corps that did not want them, these men deserve an honored niche in Marine Corps history because they earned it. They must be remembered as the beginning of a very important legacy. A legacy to be woven into the fabric of what is now called American History so that the phrase "A Marine" will come closer to reflecting historical fidelity.

In the opinion of Sergeant Major Huff, the first black Marine to complete thirty years of regular service: "The Marine Corps has been good to me and I feel I have been good to the Marine Corps."[48]

Chronology of Significant Events

The colors for the world's most complete Marine Corps Amphibious Training Base, Camp Lejeune, which was under final stages of construction, were raised at Montford Point located on the banks along New River, N.C. At that time, few people knew about Montford Point, separated from the main camp by twelve miles of pine forest. The "green huts" at Montford Point became the home base for more than 20,000 Black Marines. Events during this period were rapidly developing. Hundreds of white regulars Marines were asked to volunteer their experience and service to help train the new black recruits.

After Executive Order #8802 was issued, thousands of black men volunteered their service for the United States Marine Corps. They came from all walks of life to serve their country during the dark days of 1942. Black recruits arrived daily. Draft Boards were requested to send their most capable prospects. There were college graduates, specialized technicians, public school teachers, some relinquishing commissions in the Army, ROTC graduates and other qualified professionals. Montford Point was originally constructed for the initial quota of 1200 recruits; but as the number increased, the site was considerably expanded. Five different commands were maintained there during the war period, Recruit Depot, Headquarters, Steward Branch, Defense Battalion and a separate Infantry Battalion with attached Depot and Ammunition Companies which ably assisted in landing operations of the Fleet Marine Force.

In the Recruit Depot Battalion every "boot" received basic training similar to that of Leathernecks at Parris Island, S.C. and San Diego, Ca. History will note later that there were not two Recruit Depots in the Marine Corps, but three, often omitted from historical annals. At first, white non-commissioned officers had charge of recruit drilling, but some black noncoms among the ranks succeeded in taking over the responsibilities. There were no commissioned officers among the blacks, but several attained top-ranking NCO status, including Sergeant Majors.

The 51st Composite Defense Bn. became the pace setter and yardstick by which can be measured the progress of the Black Marine. The 52nd was patterned along similar lines. Practically every weapon handled by Black Marines on land or seas was studied by the Montford Point elite. At special schools they became familiar with the construction, maintenance and functions of weapons varying from .30 calibre cartridges to 155mm shells. Defense Battalions broke existing coastal and anti-aircraft firing records.

Adapting themselves expertly to military life and procedures, they were woven into hard-hitting infantry, defense, depot, ammunition, artillery, antiaircraft, seacoast artillery and specialized weapons group. Landing operations were conducted under simulated combat conditions.

Visitors praised the high morale and military courtesy at their camp, reflecting the behavior of the Marines when they traveled to other parts of the region. "They're so damn proud to be Marines" a white officer explained. An exceptionally smart appearance was made on their parade grounds; marching in characteristic rhythm to the music of their fine band, few services could equal theirs in military dignity and public inspiration. Before his death, late Secretary of the Navy, Frank Knox, attended one of their programs and was lavish in his praise. Their esprit de corps was exemplified not only in their military training, specialized schools and educational pursuits, but also in their religious services, their fine choir, and in their recreational activities, with their outstanding baseball, basketball and boxing teams.

The Black Marines wore the globe and anchor proudly and so did 21,609 other men who went through Montford Point Camp. The great majority proved it overseas, others at the Naval Ammo Depot out in McAlester, Oklahoma, and still others at the Philadelphia Supply Depot. Colonel Samuel A. Woods, first C.O. of the "special duty" units that were created and trained at Montford Point was justly proud of his marines and his association with all Black Marines. Said, General Leonard F. Chapman Jr., later Commandant of the Marine Corps:

> The footprints of Montford Point Marines were left on the beaches of Roi-Namur, Saipan, Guam, Peleliu, Iwo Jima and Okinawa. Tide and wind have, long ago, washed them out into the seas of history, but, "The Chosen Few" in field shoes and canvas leggings, also left their mark in the firm concrete of Marine Corps spirit. And, as new generations of Marines learn to match those footprints, their cadence assumes the proud stride of the men from Montford Point.

1941—On June 25, FDR issued Executive Order #8802, Fair Employment Practice Commission which directed the Armed Forces of the U.S. to accept all recruits "regardless of color, race, creed or national origin." First Lady Eleanor Roosevelt, A. Phillip Randolph, President of the Brotherhood of Sleeping Car Porters Union, Lester B. Granger, Executive Director of the National Urban League and Special Advisor to Navy Secretary James Forrestal were notable supporters of this order.

Granger's recommendation for integration of Naval and Marine Corps recruitment played a major role in the eventual desegregation.

1942—June 1, the Marine Corps began recruitment of black enlistees. Montford Point Camp, Camp Lejeune, New River, N.C. (original site of the Civilian Conservation Corps) amidst a dense Carolina pine forest, infested with mosquitoes, snakes and bears was established as the recruit depot and advanced training facility for all black marine enlistees.

James E. "Jimmy" Stewart, Sr., of Oklahoma City, Oklahoma, was responsible for the first black to be recruited and sworn in the USMC. Stewart himself eventually enlisted shortly after.

On August 26th, Howard Perry of Charlotte, N.C., was the first black recruit to arrive at Montford Point Camp.

H&S Battery of 51st Composite Defense Bn. was activated, Colonel Samuel A. Woods, C.O.

In Sept. the "Mighty" 1st, 2nd and 3rd Recruit Platoons of forty men each was formed.

In November, initial recruit platoons end eight weeks of Boot Camp, thus the first modern-day Black Marine graduates. Following were the first Black Marine drill instructors: Egdar R. Huff,

Thomas Brokaw, Charles E. Allen, Gilbert h. Johnson, Arnold R. Bostic, Mortimer A. Cox, Edgar R. Davis, Jr., and George A. Jackson (former U.S. Army 2nd Lt.).

1943—January 10th, activation of 1st Marine Depot Co.
  March 8th, activation of 1st Ammunition Co.
  December 15th, activation of 52nd Defense Bn.

1944—Ivan R. Elmore of Washington, D.C., appointed Camp's Band Drum Major and Bandmaster of the Montford Point Band.
  June 15th, 3rd Ammo, 18th, 19th and 20th Marine Depot Companies landed and engaged in fierce attacks with the enemy on Saipan and Tinian Islands in the Marianas. All elements were awarded the Presidential Unit Citation.
  July 21st, the 2nd and 4th Marine Ammo Companies landed on Guam, Marianas Islands. Cited for heroism and bravery, awarded the Navy Unit Commendation. Luther Woodward of 4th Ammo cited with Bronze Star.
  September 15th, the 7th Ammo and 11th Depot Companies took part in the struggle for Peleliu, Palau Islands with the Marine Division.

1945—February 19th, the 8th Marine Ammo and 36th Marine Depot Companies landed on D–Day with elements of the First Amphibious Corps on Iwo Jima, Volcanoe Islands. The and 34th landed on the 24th. Privates James M. Whitlock and James Davis of the 36th, received the Bronze Star for "heroic achievements in connection with operations against the enemy." All units of the Fifth Amphibious Corps were awarded the Navy Unit Commendation. Said Admiral Chester Nimitz, Chief of Naval Operations: "Uncommon valor was a common virtue."
  April 1st, Invasion of Okinawa, Ryuky Islands where the largest number of Black Marines served in combat. 1st, 3rd and

12th Ammo Co's; 5th, 18th, 37th, 38th Depot Companies, followed later with the 9th, 10th, 19th and 20th Depots.

Harry Lee Wright was first Black Marine to attain the rank of
Sergeant Major.

November 10th, PFC Frederick C. Branch of Philadelphia was
commissioned as a Reserve Officer in the U.S. Marine Corps, thus
becoming the 1st Black to attain distinction.

September, occupation of Japan at Sasebo Naval Base, Forces
included the 24th, 33rd, 34th, 42nd, 43rd Depot Co's., 6th, 8th
and 10th Ammo Co's. The 36th followed in Oct. In Tsingtao,
China the 12th Ammo and 20th Depots. In Tientsin, China the
1st Ammo and the 5th, 37th and 38th Depots assisted in the
Occupational campaign.

1946—Last Recruit Platoons at Montford Point Camp, 573, 574
575th.; Montford Point trained 19,168 with 12,738 serving overseas during World War II. Only 7 of 12 Ammo Co's and 12 of 51
Depots saw combat in the war.

1948—Executive Order #9981 issued by President Harry S.
Truman ending color bias in the American armed forces.

1949—June 23rd, ALNAV 49–447, Secretary of Navy Francis P.
Matthews issued "Equal opportunity for all personnel in the
Navy/Marine Corps without regard of race, color religion or
national origin."

Sept. 8th, First Black Woman Marine Annie E. Graham
enlisted at Detroit, Michigan.

Sept. 9th, Montford Point Camp was deactivated. Sgt Charles
Shaw, USMC became First Black Marine Drill Instructor at Parris
Island Recruit Depot.

Warrant Officer Annie L. Grimes of Chicago became First
Black Woman Marine Officer.

1950—First integrated unit to see combat at Pusan, Korea (First Provisional Marine Brigade).

2nd Lt.. Wm. K. Jenkins, USMCR of Elizabeth, N.J., called to active duty in Korea. Later became the first black officer to lead Marines in combat, both as a weapons and rifle platoon commander with Co. B, 1st Bn., 7th Marines.

1952—October, 2nd Lt. Frank E. Petersen, Jr., became first black marine pilot.

1954—Edgar R. Huff became the first black infantry battalion sergeant major.

1968—On March 12th, Colonel Samuel A. Woods, Jr., USMC (Ret.) died in Phoenixville, Pa. Was First C.O. at MPC.

May 12th, Sgt. Maj. Aggripa W. Smith, 1st Bn., 9th Marines, received Presidential Unit Citation on behalf of his Bn. This was presented at the White House by President Lyndon B. Johnson for outstanding combat performance at Khe Sanh. Smith was also awarded the Bronze Star for gallantry and, promoted later as Sgt. Maj. of 26th.

1969—January 1st, Lt. Col. Hurdle L. Maxwell, 1st Bn., 6th Marines was first black officer to command an infantry battalion.

1970—On Jan. 1st, Sgt. Maj. Louis Roundtree, USMC retired after twenty-two years of service. Served in Korea and Vietnam, was recipient of three Silver Stars, four Bronze Stars with Combat V, three Purple Hearts and seventeen other awards. Total of twenty-seven military decorations.

1972—Aug. 5th, Sgt. Maj. Gilbert H. Johnson, USMC (Ret.) died of a coronary attack while delivering a major address before the audience of a Montford Point reunion at Camp Lejeune, N.C.

Sept. 28th, Sgt. Maj. Edgar R. Huff, USMC, first Black Marine to complete thirty years of regular service, also having held the rank of Sgt. Major longer than any active duty Marine.

1973—Colonel Herbert L Brewer, USMCR of San Antonio, Texas, highest ranking black officer in the Marine Reserve.

Honorable James E. Johnson, CWO (Ret.) an original Montford Point enlistee, was appointed as Asst. Secretary of the Navy for Manpower Reserve Affairs.

1974—April 19th, Montford Point Camp was renamed Camp Johnson in honor of the late Sgt. Maj. Gilbert H. Johnson, USMC. Only U.S. Military installation named in honor of a Black American. Sgt. Maj. Johnson throughout his illustrious career drove relentlessly on the Black American to succeed academically. He was a soldier, seaman prior to his service as a Marine. "Hashmark" as he was appropriately called, was indeed proud of the accomplishments of the Blacks in the Marine Corps. On the basis of his devotion to Corps and country, a recommendation was made by the Association's Council members, endorsed by Asst. Secretary of the Navy Johnson, the CMC General Cushman approved the renaming of Montford Point Camp. Truly, a deserving tribute to a distinguished human being and all Blacks who have worn the eagle, globe and anchor.

Medal of Honor recipients (Posthumously).

For conspicuous gallantry and intrepidity at the risk of his life above and beyond the call of duty:

PFC James Anderson, Jr., USMC (First Black Marine recipient); PFC Robert R. Jenkins, Jr., USMC; PFC Oscar P. Austin, USMC; PFC Ralph H. Johnson, USMC; Sgt. Rodney M. Davis, USMC.

1979—Colonel Frank E. Petersen, USMC of Topeka, Kansas was confirmed by the U.S. Senate on March 12th to be promoted to the rank of Brigadier General. First Black to attain a star in the U.S. Marine Corps. Previously, General Petersen was awarded the OFC in Korea, many other coveted awards for service in Vietnam; commanded a fighter attack squadron, making him the first Naval Black Officer to lead a tactical air squadron.

1980—On May 29th, Captain Charles F. Bolden Jr., USMC (now Col.) was appointed a space shuttle pilot in the NASA program. Became First Black Marine Astronaut. Also served as National's MPMA PRO in 1975.

1981—First Sergeant William (Jack) McDowell, USMC (Ret.) was awarded the Bronze Star (updated later to Silver Star) for valor and heroic achievements while serving with the 9th Marines in South Vietnam. As a result of wounds sustained in both Korea and Vietnam conflicts, he is recipient of three Purple Hearts. Currently serves as MPMA's PRO.

1982—Captain Thomas Haywood McPhatter, USN, Chaplain Corps attained highest rank in naval service of any Montford Pointer. Served in USMC (1943–1946). Was participant in the fierce struggle for Iwo Jima while serving with the 8th Field Depot. Was Association's VP during 1975.

1984—Colonel Jerome Gary Cooper, USMCR from Mobile, Alabama was promoted to Brigadier General in the Marine Reserve.

1985—USS Rodney M. Davis, a missile frigate was commissioned at Long Beach, Ca. First named after a Black American Medal of Honor recipient.

1986—June 19th, twenty years and five days of active duty, Lt. Col. Joseph H. Carpenter, USMCR, retired. He was last of active duty Marines originally graduated from Recruit Depot, MPC.

1988—HMC announced the retirement of Lt. General Frank E. Petersen, USMC. The General, a jet fighter pilot and combat veteran of the Korean and Vietnam Wars, became the Corps' first active duty Black General in 1979.

Since July, 1986, he has served as the Chief of the Marine Corps Combat Development Command at Quantico, Va. Was the Navy's "Grey Eagle" and the Pentagon's senior aviator. The General was designated a pilot in Oct. '52, becoming the Corps' first Black aviator.

Change of Command/Retirement Ceremonies were held on July 8th at Lejeune Field, MCCOC, Quantico, Virginia.

1989—Brigadier General Jerome G. Cooper was promoted to Major General, USMCR.

At present there are no Black Generals serving as Regular Active-Duty with the USMC.

Twenty years following World War II during the month of Aug. 1965 a reunion was organized by a group of enterprising Marine veterans and active-duty Marines from Philadelphia. The purpose was to renew old friendships and share experiences of former comrades who were trained at Recruit Depot, Montford Point Camp, Camp Lejeune, New River, N.C. This group, chaired by Master Gunnery Sergeant Brooks E. Gray, USMC, held a meeting in Philadelphia, Pa., formulated and developed plans to hold a National Reunion. The response was overwhelming and consequently four hundred Marines from all over the country convened at the Adelphia Hotel in Philadelphia; hence the establishment of the Montford Point Marine Association, a non-profit Veterans' organization; subsequently chartered in Pennsylvania, 1966. Brooks E. Gray (founding father) was elected as the association's first national president.

Today the Association has eighteen bona-fide Chapters throughout the various regions of the U.S. and a Ladies Auxiliary boasting several chapters. The MPMA, Inc. is an affiliate member of the Marine Corps Council (a family council of Marine Veteran groups). Annual reunions are held to affirm their bonds to the U.S. Marine Corps; present awards and testimonials; expand its interest and service in civic programs; provide fiscal scholarship support and other benevolent essentials.

Our creed amply reflects "To promote and preserve the strong bonds of friendship born from shared adversities and to devote ourselves to the furtherance of theses accomplishments to insure more peaceful times." For our fallen comrades, servicemen and servicewomen in other branches of the military, who sacrificed their lives for the defense and freedom of America, we pay a special homage, now and in the future. For their worthy sacrifices we proudly express, "Semper Fidelis."

Black Marine Units
of the Fleet Marine Force, World War II

Date of Activation	Unit Designation	Date of Deactivation	Where Deactivated
18 Aug 1942	51st Composite Def Bn	31 Jan 1946	Montford Point
8 Mar 1943	1st Marine Depot Co	4 Jan 1946	Montford Point
23 Apr 1943	2d Marine Depot Co	4 Jan 1946	Montford Point
23 Apr 1943	3d Marine Depot Co	4 Jan 1946	Montford Point
1 June 1943	4th Marine Depot Co	31 Oct 1943	Guam
8 Jul 1943	5th Marine Depot Co	31 Oct 1943	New Caledonia
8 Jul 1943	6th Marine Depot Co	31 Aug 1943	New Caledonia
16 Aug 1943	7th Marine Depot Co	11 Dec 1945	Montford Point
16 Aug 1943	8th Marine Depot Co	10 Dec 1945	Montford Point
15 Sep 1943	9th Marine Depot Co	31 Dec 1945	Montford Point
15 Sep 1943	10th Marine Depot Co	22 Dec 1945	Montford Point
1 Oct 1943	1st Marine Ammunition Co	21 Feb 1946	Montford Point
7 Oct 1943	11th Marine Depot Co	4 Dec 1945	Saipan
7 Oct 1943	12th Marine Depot Co	11 Dec 1945	Montford Point
1 Nov 1943	13th Marine Depot Co	30 Nov 1945	Guam
1 Nov 1943	14th Marine Depot Co	30 Nov 1945	Guam
1 Nov 1943	2d Marine Ammunition Co	20 Jan 1946	Guam
1 Dec 1943	15th Marine Depot Co	30 Nov 1945	Allen Island
2 Dec 1943	16th Marine Depot Co	29 Jan 1946	Montford Point
2 Dec 1943	3d Marine Ammunition Co	25 Feb 1946	Montford Point
15 Dec 1943	52d Defense Bn	14 May 1946	Montford Point
1 Jan 1944	17th Marine Depot Co	16 Jan 1946	Montford Point
1 Jan 1944	18th Marine Depot Co	29 Jan 1946	Montford Point
1 Jan 1944	4th Marine Ammunition Co	8 Mar 1946	Guam
1 Feb 1944	19th Marine Depot Co	25 Feb 1946	Montford Point
1 Feb 1944	20th Marine Depot Co	21 Feb 1946	Montford Point
1 Feb 1944	5th Marine Ammunition Co	4 Jul 1946	Montford Point
1 Mar 1944	21st Marine Depot Co	2 Apr 1946	Montford Point
1 Mar 1944	22d Marine Depot Co	2 Apr 1946	Montford Point
1 Mar 1944	6th Ammunition Co	15 Dec 1946	Sasebo
1 Apr 1944	23d Marine Depot Co	5 Apr 1946	Montford Point
1 Apr 1944	24th Marine Depot Co	2 May 1946	Nagasaki
1 Apr 1944	7th Marine Ammunition Co	8 May 1946	Montford Point
1 May 1944	25th Marine Depot Co	2 May 1946	Montford Poin
1 May 1944	26th Marine Depot Co	2 May 1946	Montford Point
1 May 1944	8th Marine Ammunition Co	30 Sep 1947	Guam
1 Jun 1944	27th Marine Depot Co	16 Apr 1946	Montford Point
1 Jun 1944	28th Marine Depot Co	2 May 1946	Montford Point
1 Jun 1944	9th Marine Ammunition Co	4 Jul 1946	Montford Point
1 Jul 1944	29th Marine Depot Co	8 May 1946	Montford Point
1 Jul 1944	30th Marine Depot Co	8 Apr 1946	Montford Point

1 Jul 1944	10th Marine Ammunition Co	6 May 1946	Montford Point
1 Aug 1944	31st Marine Depot Co	30 Nov 1945	Maui
1 Aug 1944	32d Marine Depot Co	8 May 1946	Montford Point
1 Aug 1944	11th Marine Ammunition Co	4 Jul 1946	Montford Point
1 Sep 1944	33d Marine Depot Co	31 Jan 1946	Guam
1 Sep 1944	34th Marine Depot Co	31 Jan 1946	Guam
1 Sep 1944	12th Marine Ammunition Co	3 Apr 1946	Montford Point
1 Oct 1944	35th Marine Depot Co	6 Jun 1946	Montford Point
1 Oct 1944	36th Marine Depot Co	17 Jun 1946	Montford Point
1 Nov 1944	37th Marine Depot Co	2 Apr 1946	Montford Point
1 Nov 1944	38th Marine Depot Co	2 Apr 1946	Montford Point
1 Nov 1944	5th Marine Depot Co	21 Feb 1946	Montford Point
1 Dec 1944	6th Mairne Depot Co	31 Dec 1945	Guam
1 Dec 1944	39th Marine Depot Co	10 Jun 1946	Guam
1 Dec 1944	40th Marine Depot Co	4 May 1946	Saipan
3 Mar 1945	41st Marine Depot Co	23 Mar 1946	Maui
14 Mar 1945	42d Marine Depot Co	15 Mar 1946	Sasebo
14 Mar 1945	43d Marine Depot Co	13 Mar 1946	Sasebo
18 Apr 1945	44th Marine Depot Co	8 Apr 1946	Montford Point
10 Aug 1945	45th Marine Depot Co	6 Jun 1946	Montford Point
1 Oct 1945	46th Marine Depot Co	13 Jul 1946	Montford Point
1 Oct 1945	47th Marine Depot Co	31 Oct 1946	Oahu
1 Oct 1945	48th Marine Depot Co	10 Jun 1946	Guam
1 Oct 1945	49th Marine Depot Co	30 Sep 1947	Guam

NOTES

INTRODUCTION

[1]Maj. William Ward Burrows ltr to Lt. John Hall, dtd 8 September
1798 (Chronology File, 1798-RefSec, Hist&Mus Div,
HQMC).

THE SELECT FEW

[2]From the original draft of Sgt. Edward J. Evans "Men of Montford
Point" (Negro Marines-Published Articles, Subject File, Ref.
Sec., History & Music Div., HQMC).

[3]Maj. Gen. Thomas Holcomb testimony in Hearings of the
General Board of the Navy, dtd 23 Jan. 42, Subject:
"Enlistment of Men of Colored Race (201)" (Operational
Archives Branch, Naval Historical Center), p.18.

[4]Ibid. p. 18.

[5]R. L. Lapica, ed., Facts on File Yearbook—1942 (New York:
Persons Index on File, Inc., 1943), p. 9lM, hereafter cited as
Facts on File, preceded by the year and followed by page location.

[6]1942 Facts on File, p. l09A; Navy Department Press and Radio
Release, dtd 20 May 42 (Negro Marines Press Releases,
Subject File, Ref. Sec., History & Music Div., HQMC).

[7]Gen. Ray A. Robinson interview with Hist. Div., dtd 18–19 Mar.
68 (Oral History Collection, Hist. Div., HQMC).

[8]"Col. Cockrell Succeeds Col. Woods as CO at MP," in *Camp LeJeune Globe*, dtd 65 ep44, p. 2.

[9]G. H. Johnson interview.

[10]Mr. Obie Hall interview with Hist. Div., dtd 16 Aug. 72 (Oral History Collection, History & Music Div., HQMC), hereafter Hall Interview.

BUSINESS BEGAN

[11]G. H. Johnson interview.

[12]G. H. Johnson Interview.

[13]Battery A, 51st Composite Defense Battalion Muster Roll, Aug. 42.

[14]Personal data sheets on Sgt. Maj. Charles F. Anderson and lst Sgt. Charles W. SinMons (Negro Marine Officers, Subject File, Ref. Sec., History & Music Div., HQMC).

[15]Mr. David C. Hendricks interview with Hist. Div., dtd 7 June 72; Mr. Herman Darden, Jr., interview with Hist. Div., dtd 15 Aug. 72, hereafter Darden Interview (Oral History Collection, Hist. Div., HQMC).

[16]CO, Montford Point Camp ltr to CMC, dtd 18 May 43, Subj. "Colored Personnel, Weekly Report" (Copy in Negro Marines, Subject File, Ref. Sec., History & Music Div., HQMC).

[17]G. H. Johnson Interview.

[18]G. H. Johnson Interview; Hall interview.

[19]CMC remarks at Montford Point Marine Association's 25th Anniversary Testimonial Dinner, Sheraton Park Hotel, Washington, D.C., dtd 20 Apr. 68 (CMC Speech File, Ref. Sec., History & Music Div., HQMC).

51ST DEFENSE BATTALION

[20]Commanding Officer, 51st Composite Battalion ltr to CMC, dtd 5 May 1943, Subj: Change of Organization, 51st Composite Defense Battalion (2385/40–51 File, 51st Composite Defense Battalion, Central Files, HQMC).

[21]T/O E–410, Defense Battalion, arrived 25 June 1943 (Ref. Sec., History & Music Div., HQMC).

[22]News Release, Public Relations Office, Camp Lejeune, Sep. 43 (Negro Marines, Press Release File, Ref. Sec., History & Music Div., HQMC) Casualty Card of Cpl. Gilbert Fraser, Jr. (Ref. Sec. History & Music Div., HQMC).

[23]7th Def. Bn. War Diaries and History, Dec. 40–Mar. 44.

[24]CMC ltr to CO, 51st Def. Bn., dtd 25 May 44, Subject: Marine Corps and Government Property, waste, misuse, pilferage, and vandalism of (Negroes in the Armed Forces File, Central Files, HQMC).

[25]Col. Curtis W. LeGette ltr to CO, 51st Def. Bn. dtd 27 June 44, Subject: Record of the Proceedings of an Investigation Conducted at Headquarters, 51st Defense Battalion in The Field, By Order of the Commanding Officer, 51st Defense Battalion, To inquire into alleged damages to Marine Corps and Government Property formerly on charge to the 51st Defense Battalion, U.S. Marine Corps (Negroes in the Armed Forces File, Central Files, HQMC).

[26]Stephenson letter.

[27]Hall interview.

VIETNAM

[28]Huff Interview.

[29]Program of the Camp Lejeune Chapter, Montford Point Marine Association, Fourth Annual Testimonial Dinner Honoring The Honorable Howard N. Lee, Mayor, Chapel Hill, N. C. (Negro Marines, Publications File, Ref. Sec., History & Music Div., HQMC).

[30]Assistant Secretary of the Navy (Manpower and Reserve Affairs) ltr to Mr. Grant T. Hallmon, dtd 10 Oct. 73 (Negro Marines Interview Back-up File, Ref. Sec., History & Music Div., HQMC).

[31]Camp Lejeune Globe, 25 Apr. 74.

[32]Quoted in lst Sgt. David M. Davies, "Officers Pleased with Performance of Race Fighters," Atlanta Daily World, 27 Aug. 44 (Negro Marines Press Clippings, Ref. Sec., History & Music Div., HQMC).

[33]Ibid.

[34]Quoted in "Negro Marines Win Battle Spurs: Defeated Japan's Best on Saipan," Pittsburgh Courier, 25 ep 44 (Negro Marines Press Clippings, Ref. Sec., History & Music Div., HQMC).

[35]Quoted in Camp LeJeune Globe, 6 Jan. 45.

[36]Time, 24 Jul. 44.

[37]Copies of citations filed with card files for 7th Ammunition Company and 11th Depot Company (Ref. Sec., History & Music Div., HQMC).

[38]Garand and Strobridge. Op. cit., p.710.

PROFILES OF A LEGACY

[39]Darden interview; Norfolk Journal and Guide, 4 May 46 (Negro Press Clippings File, Ref. Sec., History & Music Div., HQMC).

[40]Col. Augustus W. Cockrell ltr to Maj. Gen. Dewitt Peck, dtd 8 Jan. 45 in Sgt. Maj. Charles F. Anderson Enlisted Case File (Manpower Department, HQMC).

[41]Simmons letter.

[42]Lt. Col. Kenneth H. Berthoud, Jr., Officer's Case File (Manpower Department, HQMC).

[43]Lt. Col. Frank E. Petersen, Jr., Officer's Case File (Manpower Department, HQMC), Petersen interview.

[44]Lt. Col. Hurdle L. Maxwell official biography (Ref. Sec., History & Music Div., HQMC).

[45]Huff Interview; HQMC, Listing of Retired Marine Corps Personnel (NAVMC 1005C) Washington, 9 May 73).

[46]Huff Interview.

THE VIETNAM WAR

[47]Individual Citations and Background Data (Medal of Honor file, Ref. Sec., History & Music Div., HQMC).

[48]*Chicago Daily Defender*, 27 July 71, citing remarks by Bgen. Robert D. Bohn, USMC in an article in the August 1971 issue of *Sepia* (Negro marines Press Clippings File, Ref. Sec., History & Music Div., HQMC).

[49]Huff Interview.

INDEX

(1) Gene and Marian Doughty with General Alfred Gray USMC at the 26th Annual Leatherneck Ball.

(2) Colonel Samuel A. Woods, Jr. USMC Commanding Officer, Montford Point Camp. (USMC Photo)

(3) Lt. Colonel Floyd A. Stephenson, USMC, Commanding Officer, 51st Defense Battalion. (USMC Photo)

(4) PFC Raymond B. Floyd USMC, 51st Defense Battalion, 1943. (Photo Collins)

(5) Dr. Raymond B. Floyd Ph.D, Department Head of Counselor Education, Southern University, Baton Rouge Louisiana. (Photo Carr)

(6) Captain Robert (Bobby) Troup, USMC, Commanding Officer, 6th Marine Depot Co. Formerly of the 51st Defense Battalion, 1943. (USMC Photo)

(7) Corporal Curley McClelland, USMC, 7th Marine Ammunition Company, Peleliu Island Survivor.

(8) Robert (Bobby Troup and wife, Julie London, starts of Television Series "Emergency"). (Photo Studio)

(9) Sergeant Major Edgar R. Huff USMC. Retired 1972 after 30 years service. (USMC Photo A135412)

(10) Corporal Alvin "Tony" Ghazlo, Senior bayonet and unarmed combat instructor at Montford Point, disarms his assistant, Private Ernest "Judo" Jones. (USMC Photo 5334)

(11) Lt. Colonel Frank E. Peterson Jr. Commanding Officer, Marine Fighter Attack Squadron 314, climbs into his phantom jet for a combat mission in 1968. (USMC Photo A422355)

(12) First Black Marine pilot, 2nd Lt. Frank E. Petersen, Jr. climbs into his Corsair after arriving in Korea in April 1953. (USMC Photo A347177)

(13) First Black Marine officer Frederick C. Branch has his second lieutenants bars pinned on by his wife on 10 November 1945. (USMC Photo 500043)

(14) Second Lieutenant Gloria Smith Camp Pendleton in 1968. A Captain in 1973, she was the senior black woman officer on active duty. (USMC Photo A557862)

(15) Major Hurdle L. Maxwell, later the first black officer in command of a marine infantry battalion, in a Vietnamese village in 1966. (USMC Photo A419047)

(16) Sgt. Gene Doughty USMC, 36th Marine Depot Co. 5th Marine Division, Veteran of Iwo Jima invasion. Led the First Platoon which was awarded three Purple Hearts and two Bronze Stars for repelling a bloody Japanese attack on Iwo Jima.

(17) Colonel Herbert L. Brewer, originally commissioned in 1948, the highest ranking black officer in the Marine Corps Reserve in 1973. (USMC Photo A619582)

(18) 90MM gun crew of the 51st Defense Battalion with its gun "Lena Horne" at Eniwetok in 1945. (USMC Photo 121743)

(19) Warrant Officer Annie I. Grimes, the third black woman to enlist in the Marine Corps in 1950, is shown in 1968 with Colonel Barbara J. Bishop, Director of Women marines. (USMC Photo A416512)

(20) Lieutenant Colonel Kenneth H. Berthoud, awarded the Navy Commendation Medal with Combat "V" for Service in Vietnam in 1966.

(21) Sergeant Brenda Good, a human relations instructor, guides a discussion group of Marines from Headquarters Battalion, FMPAC. (Photo, Human Affairs Div., HQ FMFFPC)

(22) Corporal Mitchell Smith (center) Machine Gunner with Company M. 3rd Battalion, 7th Marines, Vietnam 1966. (Photo USMC 4369436)

(23) Montford Point Camp 1943. (Photo Montford Point Pictorial)

(24) PVT Fred deClouet (author), USMC 51st Defense Battalion, 1943. Retired 1984 from U.S. Justice Department. Currently lives in Denver with his wife and 2 of his 4 children.

(25) Private First Class James Anderson Jr., Medal of Honor Recipient (Posthumous). (USMC Photo A417058)

(26) Sergeant Rodney M. Davis, Medal of Honor Recipient (Posthumous). (USMC Photo A417499)

(27) Private First Class Ralph H. Johnson, Medal of Honor Recipient (Posthumous). (USMC Photo A700430)

(28) Private First Class Oscar P. Austin, Medal of Honor Recipient (Posthumous). (USMC Photo A700428)

(29) Private First Class Robert H. Jenkins, Medal of Honor Recipient (Posthumous). (USMC Photo A700433)